# UNDERSTANDING AND

# INVESTIGATING VIOLENCE

## 2ND EDITION

by

### George Seibel
Instructor Emeritus
Morton College

A Prairie Avenue Press
Criminal Justice Classic

# UNDERSTANDING AND INVESTIGATING VIOLENCE
## 2nd Edition

Manufactured in the United States of America
by OneTouchPoint-Southwest, Austin, Texas

Word Processing by
Ruth Frazen, Seal Beach, California

Cover Design by
Rebecca Byrd Arthur

PRAIRIE AVENUE PRESS
Box 217, Riverside, IL 60546
(708) 296-5724  papcj.com

Publisher's Cataloging in Publication:
SEIBEL, George 1947-
Understanding and Investigating Violence
2nd Edition

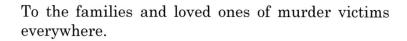

# DEDICATION

To the families and loved ones of murder victims everywhere.

May all their cases be solved.

Portions of this work contain material by the author that has appeared in other publications.

## Other Books by George Seibel

# TABLE OF CONTENTS

# INTRODUCTION: UNDERSTANDING VIOLENT BEHAVIOR

The success of any given homicide investigation often depends on the investigator's ability to interpret the killer's message. Messages vary according to motive, and it is by understanding what the killer sets out to accomplish that crimes are solved. Killers who have stalked their victims prior to the murder tend to be very consistent in their behaviors. Scorned lovers act out violence in specific ways as well.

Since most individuals are killed by someone they knew, a majority of murders are solved by conducting a thorough background investigation into the victim's past, which often results in police investigators identifying a suspect with a motive. Once the motive has been established, it is often a simple matter to develop condemning evidence against the suspect.

It is far easier to solve homicides when the victim and suspect had a pre-existing relationship, if for no other reason than the limited number of potential suspects to be sifted through. By contrast, in homicides committed by strangers, the number of potential suspects is infinite. It is, therefore, easy to understand that homicide cases with such motives as robbery, sexual attack, or twisted drives known only to the killer, are far more difficult to solve than others.

What is important to understand is that few homicide offenses with differing motives tend to contain common features. For example, stalker murders tend to be extremely overt in nature in that they are typically carried out on the public way in front of countless witnesses. Standing in direct contrast are mutilation murders, where the killer often lingers about at the crime scene while slowly inflicting wounds to an already diseased victim. Both the stalker and mutilator are extreme examples of offenders driven by rage, yet they tend to act in quite opposite manners. One crime is public in nature, the other is most private. Yet, both offenses do have one common trait; neither killer seems driven by a need to escape apprehension. The stalker commits his crime in the most public manner possible, and the mutilator shows little, if any, interest in making good his getaway from the crime scene.

Violent Pasts

Regardless of the nature of the particular crime, investigators should routinely search for violent pasts among potential suspects. Virtually all killers have come to the attention of criminal justice and social justice authorities for prior violent acts. This statement is true of both juvenile and adult offenders. Violent behavior is usually a progressive condition, whereby individuals begin acting out their anger and rage in their pre-teen years. Family members, school authorities, and the police usually learn of such violent behaviors in that sequence.

Case Study 1

A chapter is devoted to the Veronica Jefferson Case, the brutal murder of a young accountant for the CIA in 1988. The case is also treated briefly here as a means of discussing the issue of past violence on the part of homicide suspects. The facts of the case follow:

1) The victim was seen shopping in a supermarket nearby her apartment shortly before her death.
2) An off-duty police officer saw her car being driven after she left the supermarket.
3) Several hours later, her body was found in a schoolyard. She had been raped and executed.
4) The next morning, her car was found once again parked in the supermarket lot.
5) A box-cutter – as used by supermarket employees – was found inside the car.
6) Investigators therefore considered the possibility that she had been killed by an employee of the supermarket.

There were 186 employees to be considered and interviewed. Upon conclusion of that task, the investigators treated six employees as suspects. Each consented to giving blood samples for DNA comparison, and each was thusly eliminated as the killer.

Though it is not specifically known what background information the investigating police sought of the supermarket employees, it might be rightfully assumed that they did check each potential suspect for a background of violent behavior. When an individual suspect is known to have committed acts of violence in the past, they should be considered a prime suspect until such time that the subsequent investigation clears them of the crime. Similarly, the lack of a violent past should serve as a strong indication that a given suspect is probably innocent in the pending case.

Case Study 2

A drive-by shooting occurred on a busy public street. The apparent target, a noted street gang member, was gunned down as were two small children playing on their bikes. Witnesses described the car as being a metallic purple Olds with neon lights all around the lower portion of the car. However, witnesses were able to provide little in the way of a description of the occupants of the car.

Police investigators did a fine job of locating an auto, which fit the highly distinctive description of the auto. After conducting a short stakeout, the police were able to apprehend a young Hispanic man as he entered the purple Olds. He was arrested and taken to investigative headquarters for questioning.

The suspect stated that he knew nothing about the crime, nor had he allowed anyone else to drive his car. The police investigators responded by loudly threatening the suspect with the death penalty. That statement served to bring an end to the police questioning.

A second team of investigators was brought into the case. They soon learned that the suspect:

12

1) Had never been arrested for a violent act;
2) Was clearly not a member of any known street gang; and
3) Was apparently a responsible husband and father and had the same job for five years.

The new investigators made mention that the suspect's lack of a violent history – along with a lack of street gang affiliation – should be considered a huge "red flag," that he was a most unlikely prospect to be linked to a triple-murder. The initial investigators remained steadfastly convinced of his guilt, despite the only evidence against him being his purple car.

The second team of investigators convinced the suspect that they needed to know "his side of the story." It was soon learned that the suspect had been at work at the time of the crime, and before many more hours, the investigators had determined that a coworker had lifted the car keys from the suspect's work locker, then made a duplicate set, which he passed along to his brother, an infamous street gang member. On the night of the crime, the car was taken from the employee parking lot, used in the shooting, and then returned to its original parking place. To the same extent that a violent background may act to link a guilty suspect to a crime, the lack of a violent past acts to raise serious doubt about the probability of an individual's guilt in a violent crime.

Simply put, individuals do not awake one day as teens or young adults and decide to embark upon a crime of violence for the first time.

Similarly, violent behavior is enough of an integral part of one's personality that it is highly improbable that such prior acts might have gone unnoticed by the authorities.

Stalking Murders

The legal terminology of stalking varies somewhat between the states; however, the following may serve to describe the act. Stalking occurs when a victim is threatened with at least one of the following:
1) Physical harm;
2) Sexual harm;
3) Physical confinement.

The threats may be either verbalized or implied. The elements of the crime are then completed when the suspect follows or watches the victim on at least two subsequent occasions.

When stalking behavior leads to murder, certain of the following characteristics of the crime may be expected to be present.
1) The crime occurs extremely quickly, usually without prior conversation of the part of the suspect.
2) The offense may occur on the public way, or often at the victim's workplace.
3) There is seldom, if ever, a sexual component to the crime.
4) A firearm is almost always the weapon used.
5) The suspect seldom formulates a plan of action to escape arrest.

Taken together, these features make it clear as to why most murders committed by stalkers are quickly solved. The usual history of a stalking incident includes prior arrests – often first for making threats – and later, for specific stalking charges. Cases dealing with such features are also often accompanied by courts issuing either a restraining order, or an order of protection, both of which are means of legally keeping the suspect geographically away from the victim. When such court orders are established, the police are notified, and therefore, authorities usually become quite familiar with the nature of the case long before the murder occurs.

In many instances, the police are able to arrest the stalking killer at or nearby the crime scene as little effort is usually made by the suspect to get away from authorities. However, when the suspect is able to make good his getaway, the police are usually able to piece together witness accounts of the crime, along with their own prior knowledge of the stalker, so that both the motive and the identity of the killer are almost immediately established. Therefore, such crimes are normally solved within a short time period, especially in comparison to other types of murders.

General Motive Crimes

Many murders are conflict-based, but lack the intense passion and rage of certain other categories of murder. Reasons for the crime may range from a neighbor parking an eyesore vehicle alongside the killer's flower garden, to a merchant raising the price of chocolate milk, or an argument over what to prepare for dinner. Most such murders are spontaneous in nature and are often a by-product of intoxication on the part of the suspect, the victim, or both.

Such crimes might occur either in a public setting, or in the privacy of a residence, and usually occur as an immediate response to the conflict. A single weapon is typically used, and the killer is usually preoccupied with hurrying from the crime scene in order to avoid detection.

Such killers generally do have violent pasts; however, the prior acts of violence tend to have also been spontaneous outbreaks – often driven by alcohol or drugs – more than other types of violent attacks such as armed robberies or sex offenses.

Incidents of domestic abuse tend to be repetitive in nature and are often fed by addiction problems. Family conflicts often continue along similar lines with the same complaints repeating themselves again and again. Each new incident adds fuel to the fire, then the addition of a state impaired by alcohol or drugs places the potential killer over the edge due to the attacker's reduced inhibitions.

This type of murder accounts for a significant percentage of all homicide incidents. They are normally easily solved as police quickly learn about the conflict that led to the crime. Such suspects also tend to readily discuss the crime with the police, so confessions are common.

Robbery-Related Murders

Within the criminal subculture, status is awarded based on the nature of the deviant acts

16

committed by its members. Just as musical prowess and athletic achievements are sources of pride and recognition, so is the work of the criminal. The more daring the crime, the greater is one's status within the criminal community. Within this framework, the work of the armed robber is placed just below that of only the police-killer in terms of esteem and recognition from street criminals.

The term used on the street for exhibiting courage or nerve in the course of the commission of criminal acts is "heart." The individual who packs a firearm and enters the supermarket and leaves with the contents of the safe possesses great heart. The task of armed robbery requires the suspect to be willing to confront danger. Though the robber himself is armed, it is implicit in the act that the risk of the robber being shot and killed, either by a resistant victim, or by responding police, is always present. Within the criminal milieu, the greater the perceived risk attached to committing the crime, the greater the status afforded to the offender.

That robbers hold high status within the criminal community is best illustrated by the fact that it is common for robbers to take snapshots of the loot successfully taken in robberies, along with the weapons and other items used in the crime, such as ski masks. The photos are then placed prominently on display as a means of memorializing the successful robbery.

Other criminals who commit less daring offenses are seen as clearly less than the equal of those with "heart." That means, among other things, that they are not allowed to congregate on the same segment of the street with home-invaders, stick-up men, and other shooters.

Wise criminals understand certain aspects of police behavior. They know, for example, that the police work far harder and longer on robberies in which a victim has been seriously injured or killed, than they do in routine offenses where only property loss has been suffered. Therefore, most armed robbers harm their victims only when they feel forced to do so, usually due to resistance on the part of the victim.

Robbery is defined as taking property from the person of another by either a threat of force, or by actual use of force. Armed robbery occurs when the suspect is armed with a dangerous weapon in the course of that crime. Home invasion is a term used to describe the armed robbery of individuals inside a dwelling. Carjacking is an act of robbery or armed robbery in which the property taken is a motor vehicle.

Robbery investigation centers upon investigators getting to know a large segment of the total pool of offenders. By gathering mug shots of known offenders, it is possible for the police investigator to obtain a photo identification of the suspect, sometimes within a matter of moments after the commission of an offense. It then becomes a simple matter of locating the suspect who is then arrested and placed in a police line-up for the purpose of gaining a positive, in-person identification, which is usually adequate evidence to get the suspect charged. This investigative process is made easier by the fact that most inner-city robbers do not move about to commit their crimes. Most robberies are committed by suspects who reside in the immediate area of the offense.

However, robbery murders are often the work of a small segment of armed robbers who have a sadistic side and will injure or kill their victims upon completion of the robbery aspect of the crime, even when the victim follows the robber's directions to the letter.

A second issue that makes many investigations difficult rests in the fact that there is an entirely different set of robbery-murders in which robbery is not the primary motive for the crime, but rather it is merely an afterthought to killing the victim.

Case Study 3

Janet Benoit was found murdered in her motel room in Santa Fe, New Mexico. She was resting face-down on a bed with her hands bound behind her with strips of a torn pillowcase. She suffered a major stab wound in the back and multiple stab wounds to the neck. The motel room had not been ransacked, and the killer did not take the keys to her car or to the U-Haul trailer, which contained most of her belongings. A certain amount of cash remained in her purse, and some of the jewelry was still in place. However, some cash and several pieces of jewelry were taken n the course of the crime. Thus, there was a robbery element to the crime, yet robbery clearly was not the killer's primary motive.

The ability to recognize primary motive is key toward case solution, as an investigative decision to center the investigation of Janet Benoit's murder upon known armed robbers would likely have been extremely time-consuming and would have ultimately been a fruitless endeavor.

Crimes with a Sexual Component

Sex offenders may generally be categorized according to one primary aspect of method of operation, whether they carry out their acts out of doors on the public way or in the course of illegal entries into a dwelling. Though sex offenders are compulsive criminals who tend to continually act out until caught by authorities, they nonetheless seldom stray from a single method of operation.

Case Study 4

In the course of investigating the Oak Park, Illinois, murder of Karen Phillips, the author searched for other possible crimes that might have been committed by her killer. It was learned that, over Memorial Day weekend in 1978, another young woman named Rita Hopkinson was killed in a train station slightly more than a mile south of where Karen Phillips was later killed inside her apartment. The Hopkinson attacker had apparently confronted her with a knife and forced her to disrobe from the waist down; however, before the actual sex attack could occur, he was interrupted by the arrival of another passenger to the train station. The attacker mortally wounded the intruder, then chased and stabbed Rita Hopkinson to death.

The killer was never caught, however, that is not to say that police lacked clues and leads to follow. The day after the murder, a suspect who closely resembled the killer hopped a fence into a yard and raped a woman as she sunbathed. Over the succeeding years, more than thirty other women were sexually attacked by a suspect who was described as clean-cut in appearance, and who engaged his victims in intelligent and refined conversation.

What are most significant are issues of method of operation. The offenses all took place out of doors during warm-weather months between May and October. The six-year-long pattern of crimes culminated in August, 1984, with the rape-murder of Kathleen Lombardo, who was killed as she went jogging only blocks away from her home. Witnesses told police that, as she moved toward an alley where the crime took place, the clean-cut suspect dressed in jogging gear began trailing her on foot. Ten minutes later, they heard screams coming from the alley, and the victim's body was found.

Investigators assigned to the Lombardo case readily admitted to the press that the description of the killer was "practically identical to that of a rapist who had struck four times in the late-summer of 1982 in precisely the same area of Oak Park where the Lombardo crime occurred. What they did not say, however, was that the description

21

of the Lombardo suspect was also identical to that of a multiple sex offender who had been given the name of "the jogger rapist" after having committed a dozen offenses during the late-summer of 1978.

Case Analysis

As discussed elsewhere, it is quite possible that the same individual killed both Rita Hopkinson and Kathleen Lombardo. Their having been killed in the course of an intended sexual attack would be in keeping with the suspect's general method of operation. In the first incident, it is clear that the intended sexual attack of Rita Hopkinson was not consummated only because of the suspect being interrupted by the arrival of the second victim. Hypothetically, the same suspect might have committed scores of sexual offenses as suggested, and none of those would have led to the murder of the victim, providing that the suspect kills only when he meets resistance. This possible theory is imperfect to the extent that the actual dynamics of the interaction between the suspect and Kathleen Lombardo in the alley where she was attacked is not known.

In the event that she complied with the knife-wielding suspect's orders and was killed anyway, then the probability is that her killer was not the serial rapist who allowed his many rape victims to live. However, if Kathleen Lombardo failed to follow directions, or physically resisted, then the theory that one individual killed both young women remains sound. Similarly, a variation of the same concept might have been that a third person might have come along, as in the Hopkinson case, and in some way interrupted the crime.

The concept of suspects attacking their victims is well founded within the study of robbery offenders. A small percentage will not harm their victims even if they were to meet great resistance. Those offenders are simply not well suited for the task of armed robbery and would themselves flee before they might turn a weapon on their victim. The largest groups of robbers wish for their criminal work to go smoothly and, therefore, do not wish to injure their victims, for they know that the police investigate such crimes with far greater effort than more routine robberies where nobody has been injured. This category of robber will bring physical harm to their victim only when they meet resistance. This typology of robbers is completed by the sadist who first warns his victim against resistance, gains the victim's compliance, and then injures or kills them anyway.

There are the same types among sex offenders as well. The same offender might have killed both Rita Hopkinson and Kathleen Lombardo because of having been met with some form of resistance, but also might have carried out the countless other sexual attacks in between in which none of those victims were either injured or killed. Within the eyes of the suspect, there was no reason to use his knife on victims who did just as they were told. There exists, however, another type of sex offender who accounts for a large percentage of serial killers. Their description follows shortly.

This theory dealing with a serial rapist and killer gains support from both the common physical description of the suspect, along with a common method of operation in that all of the crimes took place out of doors and during warm weather months. Unfortunately, the validity of the theory remains largely a matter of speculation in that no cold case investigation has taken place, which might either prove the theory to be unsound or lead to the identification of the suspect.

Summary of Killer Categories

In general terms, about one-half of all the homicides are cleared by arrest each year in the United States. While it is impossible to determine just what percentage of murders from each of the categories discussed are actually solved, it is safe to state that more than one-half of the categories of killers discussed above are solved.

The simple fact that most homicide victims are killed by someone they knew makes those cases easier to solve than others. Robbery-murders are often solved by virtue of the fact that such killers often openly brag about their work, which results in an informant sharing that information with the police. Stalkers are nearly always caught in that their past threats toward their victim stands as loud evidence of motive once the stalking turns to murder. Sex offenders who killed due to their victim's resistance, or some other complicating factor are usually also caught simply because sex offenders comprise such a small pool of criminal suspects. If a given community might have five active rapists working in the area, there are probably fifty or more robbers. It is therefore by sifting through a very limited number of potential suspects, that rape-murder of this type are solved. These are the "easy" murders to solve. Since most homicide investigations identify one of the above categories of suspects as the wanted individual, it is logical that most police investigators focus on such types to solve whatever homicide they are investigating. However, a significantly large percentage of the homicides that are never solved do not fit into any of the above categories, and that may be the very reason that they are not solved.

Murders without Obvious Motive

Most killers know their victims. Most killers hurry through the commission of the crime in order to place distance between themselves and their crime. And, in many murders, the killer speaks of his motive through significant facts surrounding both the crime scene and the manner in which the crime was accomplished.

However, a very large percentage of homicides that come to the attention of cold case investigators are appreciably different than crimes previously discussed. They are unlike other offenses in at least some of the following ways:

1)  Wounds to the victim often imply that the killer was not in any hurry to flee the crime scene.

2)  More than one cause of death is often employed.

3) Though there is often a sexual aspect of the crime, many times there are no signs of a struggle, and only semen within the victim suggests a rape has occurred.
4) The crime scene is often tidy, as if the victim had been entertaining a friend.
5) Certain property may be taken, yet other valuables are often left behind.
6) There is often no damage to entrances to the crime scene, an indication that the victim allowed the killer inside.
7) The killer often tells the victim that if they comply with instructions that they will save their life.
8) The killer then betrays the victim by killing them, despite their lack of resistance.

In many such cases, certain of these features will be present. Many times, there will also be other unusual aspects of the crime, which escape the list above. However, when some combination of the above qualities is present in a homicide, it is safe to take the position that the actual motive for the offense is simply the joy the killer derives from committing the act itself.

Four primary cases are treated in this book: the murders of Karen Phillips, Janet Benoit, Veronica Jefferson, and Rachel Raver. They are remarkable for the number of apparent similarities as to the behaviors of their respective killers.

Karen Phillips was killed in her studio apartment in Oak Park, Illinois, in 1980. She had been beaten about the head, with at least one blunt instrument, strangled, and had over forty other superficial wounds to her torso, including a bite mark to the left shoulder, and two strangely configured puncture wounds to the back. She had semen in her vaginal track, but no other signs of sexual attack.

A Bible student named Steven Linscott contacted the police to tell them about his having had a dream about a similar attack at the same time that his neighbor was being killed two doors away. He was charged with the rape and murder, convicted of the murder, and sentenced to forty years in prison. Ten years later, the state dropped all charges against Linscott on the eve of a retrial ordered by an appeals court.

The nature and extent of multiple wounds strongly indicates that Karen Phillips was killed by the type of suspect who commits many murders that come to the attention of cold case investigators; the killer with a motive known only to himself.

Janet Benoit was raped and murdered inside a motel room in Santa Fe, New Mexico, in 1983. She had been strangled, stabbed in the back through her sweater, and stabbed multiple times in the neck. At the time the body was discovered, she was dressed except for her bra, and her hands were bound behind her back, and remarkably, she, too, had a bite mark in precisely the same location as the one inflicted upon Karen Phillips.

For more than a decade, the Benoit family was told by the police that there simply were no leads, which led to the author being retained to investigate in 1995. It was quickly learned that there were actually multiple suspects, none of which had ever been properly eliminated by the police.

Veronica Jefferson was a young accountant for the CIA in Washington, D.C. Her naked body was found alongside her neatly folded clothes in a schoolyard in the early-morning hours in May, 1988. She had been raped and executed, shot point-blank in the face with a handgun.

The Jefferson case was featured on the television production, *Unsolved Mysteries*. Though their treatment of the case depicted a handsome stranger Veronica had apparently just met in a supermarket as the killer, the baffled police investigators stated that they remained convinced that the victim had been killed by a jilted lover from the victim's home state of Oklahoma.

In both the Karen Phillips and Veronica Jefferson cases, the police focused their attention on "convenient" suspects who failed to meet the profiles of individuals who go about killing in the manner of those crimes. Steven Linscott was wrongly charged in the Phillips case, despite the fact that he had absolutely no known history as a violent offender. His having contacted the police about his alleged dream simply made him an easy suspect. In the Jefferson case, the police had clearly misinterpreted case facts, failed to follow logical leads, and therefore, conveniently claimed that the crime had been committed by someone located two-thousand miles away, where the police could not be expected to know about them.

The killers in all three cases seemingly sought out their respective victims for the deliberate purpose of murder and rape. All three killers took great risks in the commission of their crimes: In the case of Phillips and Benoit, they took an exhaustive amount of time engaged in "overkill" behaviors when most other suspects would have been preoccupied with getting away from the crime scene. In the Jefferson case, the killer risked discovery by having first been seen with the victim inside the supermarket, then by forcing her into her own car at gunpoint, and driving her toward her eventual death. Moreover, Veronica Jefferson's killer was observed by an off-duty police officer between the supermarket and the crime scene, yet he chose a tactic designed to outsmart the officer, rather than to relinquish custody of his victim and flee, as most suspects would do.

A prime example of the need for a serial killer to become adaptive to his compulsions to kill is prominent in the behavior of Veronica Jefferson's killer seven months after her death.

Just as Veronica Jefferson's killer spotted her in her red shoes, then was driven to attack and kill her, he later was drawn to Rachel Raver for the same reason. So great was his compulsive rage to take Rachel's life that he undertook the major complication that she was with her boyfriend, Warren Fulton, at the time.

Undeterred, he kidnapped the couple at gunpoint and forced them to drive to an isolated area where he executed Warren with a single shot to the back of the head. As Rachel attempted fleeing on foot, she too was shot in the head before being sexually attacked.

Remarkably, the police ignored that both women wore red shoes and that both had their clothes neatly stacked alongside their bodies. They took the position that the crimes were unrelated primarily because Rachel had been with Warren Fulton when killed. Unfortunately, what was lost on the police was the adaptive nature of serial killers to modify their preferred method of operation in order to carry out their "need" to kill.

It should be understood that killers of this ilk commit their crimes simply for the joy of the act. Once this basic fact is understood, it is also possible to accept that the time-consuming aspects of their crime do not concern this type of killer as they would others. For them, the risk of being caught simply enhances their pleasure based on their ability to avoid investigative scrutiny. Mutilation and other overkill aspects of such crimes are the basis for this killer's need to act out in the first place. To inflict any less wounds would leave them short of the satisfaction commission of the act provides them. Similarly, the more time taken in the course of the crime, the greater their satisfaction at having outsmarted the police.

Such killers respond to twisted quirks that act to "trigger" their behaviors. To the extent that they are triggered to act, it is a safe assumption that this is not something that is likely to occur only once. If the long, black curly hair of Janet Benoit caused her killer to experience an inner-rage and respond by committing the crime as a result, there are clearly going to be other women – and similar conditions – where the same suspect will respond in the same manner to such stimuli and, therefore, act out in the same manner with a different victim. Make no mistake about it, to the extent that this category of killer is impulsively "triggered" to act, the behavior will be repeated in similar fashion until caught.

The Search

While there is certain to be a common thread between one crime and the next, the impulsive killer's method of operation may be less constant than among other criminal offenses. For example, if an armed robber has had success in robbing taxi drivers while posing as a passenger leaving a train station, he may use that tact time after time. The robber is able to make a logical decision to commit another robbery that results in his gathering his weapon and setting out for the place in which he has decided to identify a potential victim, and then carry out the crime in keeping with his chosen method of operation. This offender has the luxury of such extensive planning.

The impulsive killer's plight is totally different. For example, in the Veronica Jefferson case, it seems apparent that her killer saw the victim as she walked from the parking lot and into

31

the supermarket. The killer's particular "trigger" seems to have been the red shoes the victim wore. Her shoes, perhaps along with the victim's general appearance thus compelled the killer to act. He then entered the supermarket with a clear-cut plan in mind to rape the victim in the course of taking her life. Since the killer was emotionally lured to his intended victim, he did not have the luxury of the more logically inclined criminal who is able to map out a specific course of action in advance of the crime. This category of offender is forced to improvise as he moves toward the culmination of his criminal act. It is for this reason that essentially similar crimes committed by a single offender may seem on the surface to be different as the result of differing methods of operation.

When the impulsive killer acts, it should therefore be an investigative expectation that each possible serial offense will have differing aspects to them due to the spontaneous nature of having responded to something the killer saw in a potential victim.

Searching for Triggers

It is an investigative error to assume that the victims of impulsive killers are likely to all be of the same race or the same physical size or of the same age group. The psychological quirks that may activate the killer might be something as deeply hidden as the fragrance of a perfume once worn by an abusive individual, or a facial expression of someone who may, or may not, actually resemble the individual in the killer's past.

It is a common investigative error to dismiss the possibility that one suspect may have committed multiple offenses. In the Jefferson case, the police remained convinced that she was killed by a former lover, despite the fact that another young woman was killed in a similar way a short distance away seven months later. Investigators decided that two major differences between the respective cases were sufficient to assume against the presence of a common killer. Veronica Jefferson was African-American, while the second victim was White, and the second victim was killed along with her boyfriend, while Veronica had been alone.

However, what was constant in both cases was that both of the female victims wore red shoes, and the clothing of both female victims was neatly folded alongside the place where they were raped and met their death. It was not until nearly a decade later that DNA conclusively proved that the same suspect had raped – and therefore killed – both women.

Crime Location

One usual characteristic of a method of operation is the location where the crime takes place. As stated earlier, rapists usually either work indoors or outdoors. Some suspects grab their victims as they walk past the mouth of the alleys or as they enter or exit their autos in or near garages. Others lurk in the vestibules of apartment buildings in wait for potential victims to open a door toward their apartment.

A different manner of sex offender attacks after having entered a victim's home, either by means of burglary or home invasion. Police investigators have learned that very few sex offenders – who allow their victims to live after the attack – change methods of operation by committing the crimes both in and out of doors. They are like armed robbers in that they have the luxury of planning their crimes in such a way that they can be certain of just what the crime scene will be like.

The impulsive killer makes no such plans, any more than he can effectively predict just when he will be triggered toward committing another crime. It is, therefore, quite possible that one such offense might occur outside in a park, the next inside where he might have followed his victim, to be stalked by yet another attack inside an abandoned auto. The impulsive killer improvises toward the successful commission of his crime. This is therefore yet one more example of the ways in which a simple study of method of operation may totally obscure the fact that various seemingly dissimilar crimes are actually the work of a single serial killer.

Investigative Guidelines

When an overkill murder, especially one with a sexual component, is discovered, the probability is great that the suspect has killed others in the past in a way that is at least somewhat similar. *All murders in which the suspect seems to have spent a great deal of time in the course of the act should be*

34

*scrutinized.* Differences in method of operation should be disregarded, and a search should center on seeking as little as one similarity between the various crimes.

All time-consuming homicides with a sexual overtone should be considered as the work of a serial killer.

Perhaps the single most important guideline in conducting such investigations is that any two over-kill crimes committed within short proximity of one another are probably the work of a single killer. The worst thing any investigator – cold case or otherwise – can ever do is to make an arbitrary decision that the cases are unrelated without first having thoroughly investigated both crimes. The probability is overwhelmingly great that the search is actually for a serial killer.

Wounds as a Method of Operation

Despite the impulsive killer's dilemma of often having to improvise along the way as his crime is developing, there are certain killers whose crimes will bear a "trademark" in terms of the manner and nature of wounds inflicted upon the victim. Some examples are as common as strangulation by means of the victim's blouse or scarf being twisted around the neck. In other cases, the wounds may be so unusual that they set the case apart from virtually all others.

For example, Janet Benoit was stabbed multiple times in the neck. Though knife wounds to the neck are common, they are normally in the form of lacerations, thus the term "slitting one's throat." Therefore, when police gained information that another young woman in a neighboring state was also killed by stab wounds to the neck, that killer rightfully should have been considered a prime suspect in the Benoit case.

Case Study 5

A young woman was found in the warm-up house of an ice-skating rink in a well-known winter resort area. She had been strangled with a long scarf she wore around her neck. Her ski pants were in place; however, her panties were found in the woman's washroom nearby. The autopsy disclosed a presence of semen within her vaginal track, but there was no other evidence supportive of rape. There were more than sixty puncture wounds to the front of her torso, and the victim's long, blonde hair was tied together in a tight knot in a haphazard manner.

Police investigators looked into the victim's past and found that she had broken up with an individual who had continued to pursue her for many months after. He had no clear-cut alibi for the time of the crime, claiming to have been home alone at the time that the victim was killed several hundred miles away. Police spent several days attempting to locate service station attendants or train personnel who might have been able to place the suspect near the crime scene, however, no such witnesses were to be found. Investigators then subjected the former boyfriend to a rigorous line of questioning, however, the suspect continued to maintain his innocence.

Months went by, during which time the police obtained the suspect's telephone records and maintained extensive surveillance of him, in hopes that he might do something to give away his guilt. The case went unsolved for several years. The victim's family then retained a cold case investigator, who soon noted that the victim had been to a beauty salon during the last day of her life. A visit was made there at which time it was learned that the stylist who had done the victim's hair had long since moved out of state; therefore, it was not immediately possible to learn about the nature of the victim's conversation while having her hair done.

The owner of the salon, however, clearly recalled the victim having been there. The new investigator then asked whether she might recall anything unusual about the day in question. She responded that the crime took place during a stretch of time in which a "very strange homeless type" had been hanging around on the bench next to the salon. It seems that he had attempted to strike up conversation with certain salon customers as they came and went. Salon clients were afraid of him and called the police.

What was most significant about the conversation was that the salon owner was positive that she never saw the stranger again after the murder. The investigator inquired as to whether she had shared the same information with the original investigators. She stated that she had never been interviewed until that very day.

A few key pieces of information had surfaced:

1) A suspect whose behavior and demeanor were sufficient to scare women had been lurking about prior to the crime;

2) A salon might have served as a place for the killer to effectively "scout" women; and

3) He was never again seen in the area after the murder.

The new investigator had both the best and worst of it: He had a strong lead to follow, however, he also faced the difficult task of attempting to identify and locate an unknown suspect. Clearly, someone in the area was likely to have known something about the stranger at the time of the crime. But it would be a seemingly impossible task to move about the immediate community asking questions about a nameless suspect years after the fact. Note the recurring nature of this problem.

The police were contacted. In a stroke of good luck, a female officer did recall the vagrant, however, no official report was filed that might contain the suspect's name. He was a homeless drifter with bad hygiene and the only other thing the officer recalled about him was that he said that he was from Iowa. He was White, age about thirty at the time, and had a pock-marked face. The new investigator spent several more days in the area of the salon seeking more information about the suspect, but none was forthcoming.

Iowa police were told about the case. They had no leads as to the suspect, however, they did have information about an unsolved rape and murder in which the victim was apparently abducted from a public telephone in front of a convenient store. In that case, the victim was stabbed multiple times with an unknown type of weapon, which inflicted puncture wounds. The cold case investigator was also able to determine that the semen in the Iowa victim was of the same blood-typing as in the initial case. This information would be sufficient to assume that both crimes were committed by the same suspect until actual DNA typing could be accomplished.

A search was then undertaken for the suspect in shelters and other places where the homeless congregate. At each stop along the way, the investigator asked about an individual who might have been reluctant to put down his knapsack or duffel bag. At perhaps the tenth stop, an elderly woman at a soup kitchen asked how in earth it was that he knew that about a fellow. She explained that only a few months earlier just such an individual attacked another homeless person for having picked up his travel bag. "Stuck him good with an icepick, he did," she said.

As it turned out, the victim had refused to sign a complaint; however, the suspect's name was on file with the local police. Thus, the hunt for Julius Wilkes was on.

By then, it was early-May and warm weather landed in a college town the same day the cold case investigator arrived. He cruised in and out of paths leading to and from sorority houses before focusing on an individual who might have been Wilkes. He sat on a park bench leering at certain of the passing coeds. To be precise, the suspect leered only at the girls who were blonde. The investigator took a hundred dollar bill and poked a hole through it with a stick, then stuck it into the lawn a few feet away from where the suspect sat. It only took a few seconds for the suspect to see the money and lunge toward it. At that instant, the investigator grabbed the dirty green bag from the bench. Inside it was an icepick and a blonde wig with its long, fake hair tied into a knot, just like had been done to both victims in the course of their attacks.

When Julius saw his belongings spread out on the bench, he stood spellbound and began hyperventilating as handcuffs were placed on his wrists. Within a day or two, more "overkill" crimes were uncovered in nearby states. The suspect admitted to all of them.

The killer's "trigger" was formed by his first girlfriend who, after introducing him to lovemaking, mocked him by telling him about her many other lovers. His plan to kill her had become spoiled when she committed suicide, so Julius was forced to take up his cause on other attractive young women with long, blonde hair. His chosen method of operation was so vital to his crimes that he carried his weapon with him everywhere he went so that he might be "prepared" when just the right victim triggered him into action. Similarly, he carried the blonde wig with him, both as a constant reminder of his "cause," and also so that he might practice knotting the hair of his victims just so.

## Case Study 6

A man was killed inside a steam room within the men's locker room of a posh health club. The victim was one of four individuals in the steam room then two others walked in. They sat alongside the victim. Seconds later, one of the new arrivals turned toward the victim and told him that he was not supposed to be shaving in the steam room. Witnesses would later state that there was then an angry reply, apparently from the victim. One of the men who had just entered the room smashed the victim's head against the tile wall, killing him instantly. The two suspects then walked from the steam room.

Witnesses stated that the room had been too steamy to see the faces of the suspects. Police found a disposable razor on the floor of the steam room. Investigators interviewed scores of individuals seeking information about possible suspects who might have been seen dressing quickly after the crime. They also inquired about members or guests known to have bad tempers, and they inspected guest lists. They also searched for witnesses who might have seen strangers sneaking into the club. The investigators also looked into the backgrounds of club employees, seeking someone with a violent history who might have "flipped out" at the victim having been shaving in the steam room. Months later, the case remained unsolved.

The commander of the investigative unit then reassigned the case to a different team. They read the police file and immediately saw that the initial investigators had never moved beyond searching for clues centered on the health club and the killers' apparent violent reaction to the victim's practice of shaving in the steam room.

The new investigators did a thorough background check of the victim and soon learned that there were at least two parties who might have had a motive for killing him. According to the victim's mother, the widow had done very little grieving and was currently seeing a much younger fellow. The victim had also sued a former business partner only days before having been killed.

However, the notion that the victim had been killed for any reason other than the apparent conflict inside the steam room flew directly in the face of known case facts. Others inside the steam room were most certain that the altercation had seemingly been the result of a simple violation of the no shaving policy.

The new investigators began by attempting to create a theory that might account for the apparent events inside the locker room. By now, the disposable razor had been worked on at the crime laboratory. The victim's fingerprints had survived the steam of the crime scene, and the whiskers on it were also his. An examination of the crime scene photos clearly disclosed that the victim's face was completely shaved.

The investigators then constructed the following hypothesis to account for the case facts: Two individuals had reason to kill the victim that had nothing to do with shaving, however, they wished not to be caught for the crime and therefore devised a plan that might divert police attention toward a false motive.

The killers would have been familiar with the victim's schedule at the health club. They watched the victim shave. He then did one of three things with the dirty razor; he might have tossed it into the trash container, or left it atop the sink counter after finishing his shave, or perhaps he placed it back into his gym bag that was sitting beside his locker after the crime was discovered.

In any event, the killers retrieved the razor, handling it with a tissue so as not to leave their own prints and not to destroy those of the victim. The pair then followed the victim into the steam room, and then sat beside him. One suspect made the statement cautioning against shaving in the steam room, then the other suspect responded, making an angry comment of his own. The killers then immediately smashed the victim's head against the wall before he might speak. Witnesses inside the room would have logically assumed that the reply had come from the victim, and not from the suspect sitting only inches away from him. The killers then dropped the victim's razor at his feet and walked out of the steam room.

It might have happened that way and would have reasonably caused the investigators to search based on a motive that did not exist. For just as long as investigators continued to focus only on that faulty motive, the crime would remain all but impossible to solve.

The new investigators then looked carefully into the background of the victim's former business associate. There was nothing in his past to indicate a violent or otherwise criminal past. When interviewed by investigators, he stated in a matter-of-fact way that he would easily win the lawsuit that was still pending, despite the death of the victim.

The investigators then looked into the widow as a possible suspect. They soon determined that she had been frequenting a certain bar located in a nearby hotel, and that she had struck up a friendship with a known member of organized crime. The finances of the victim and widow were researched, and it was learned that several thousands of dollars had been withdrawn by the widow a week before her husband's death.

Investigators then gathered photos of known associates of the organized crime figure the widow had been seen with at the bar. They were then placed in a photo gallery and shown to employees of the health club where the murder had occurred. Both front desk and membership employees identified two suspects as having been given a tour of the club at about the same time as the steam room murder.

The widow was then confronted with that information and then quickly admitted to having put together a murder-for-hire scheme that two members of organized crime cleverly carried out by providing police investigators with a false motive in which to become lost.

This case study illustrates that the manner in which a crime occurs can logically lead investigators to a certain conclusion. When this occurs, investigators are totally correct to pursue such logic. However, after having exhausted all investigative tasks toward case solution, investigators must be sufficiently flexible to attempt to understand other ways in which the crime might have taken place.

Case Study 7

A young woman worked in a fast-food restaurant. As she and one of her employees left work early one morning, two gunmen approached them and forced them back inside the closed restaurant. The woman was then shot from point-blank range and killed. Police took the position that the murder had been the result of a robbery attempt gone wrong, and nearly three years later the crime remains unsolved.

That the police remained steadfast in their opinion that the motive for the crime had been robbery is unfortunate for several reasons. The first is that the restaurant had been closed for business for several hours at the time the gunman had arrived. The proceeds for the day had therefore been dropped into the safe long before, and the victim had no access to the money. Secondly, the victim had been working in the kitchen area away from any windows, so would-be robbers could not have looked inside and have seen the employees within. Thirdly, the victim was shot within only a matter of seconds of having been forced inside by the killers, therefore, the gunman would have hardly had time to learn that there was no money to be had by the time the shooting occurred.

Then, on the day of the victim's funeral, her own mother died in a bathtub at the victim's apartment where the widower was present. Either she died of natural causes, which would be highly coincidental, or she died by some other means. Finally, the widower was involved in a highly public relationship with a teenaged girl within a matter of days of the death of his late-wife, and he also purchased an expensive luxury auto.

The noted features of the crime effectively argue against the theory that the victim was killed in the course of a robbery attempt, and the other aspects surrounding the crime raise the issue that the motive for the crime was something other than robbery.

Since the police have never seen fit to search for alternate motives, it is impossible to know the truth about what actually occurred. However, as in the steam room, a husband wishing to be rid of his wife would have been smart in having the crime occur in the workplace, thus providing the investigators with a faulty assumed motive for the crime.

# CASE 1

## WHEN STUCK, START OVER

<u>Investigative Overview</u>
A man was killed in the steam room of a health club in an apparent fit of rage on the part of the attacker. Police investigators searched long and hard for the killer among club members and guests to no avail. Before long investigators were stuck. None of the generally effective investigative tasks had produced as much as a single suspect.
<u>Investigative Rule #1 is When Stuck, Start Over</u>.
Bright investigators know that when theories and motives are essentially correct, cases usually come together quickly. By comparison, when nothing links as it should, chances are great that the initial theory was wrong to begin with. Time to start over.

The Crime

Jonathan Pelzer was a wealthy real estate tycoon living in a major city. He and his wife, Mimi, were well known in society circles; photos of them at countless charity events often found their way to newspapers. Pelzer had made a name for himself a decade earlier as a majority owner of a Major League baseball team.

On the day of his death Pelzer had a number of business appointments atop his penthouse office overlooking the lake. He then drove the two miles to a posh health club where he worked with his personal trainer, Wendy Winn. Pelzer then entered the men's locker room and dropped his workout clothes alongside his locker and made his way to the steam room.

The victim was one of four individuals in the steam room, then two others entered as well. They then sat on either side of Pelzer. Seconds later one of the new arrivals stated that the victim was not supposed to be shaving in the steam room. A voice quickly let go with a volley of vulgarities aimed at the individuals complaining about the shaving issue. It was then that one of the men smashed the victim's head against the tile wall behind where he was sitting killing him instantly. The two suspects then calmly walked from the steam room.

The three men who had been present during the crime lingered inside the steam room fearing a confrontation with the killers should they have followed immediately. Each would tell the police the same account. The steam had been so dense that it was impossible to have seen anything more than a vague outline of either the victim or his killers. All agreed that the confrontation about shaving had taken place within seconds of the killers' arrival. There was nothing distinguishable about the voice of the killer who had confronted the victim, and none of the witnesses had known the victim prior to the crime.

The Crime Scene

Jonathan Pelzer had been naked when killed and had been sitting on a health club towel when killed. The key to his locker was pinned to the towel. A disposable razor was found on the floor beneath the bench where the killing had taken place. Pelzer was freshly shaved, and the whiskers clogging the razor blade edge would later be DNA tested disclosing that the whiskers were indeed the victim's. The handle was clean of fingerprints, apparently due to the intense moisture within the steam room.

Early Investigation

Investigators interviewed scores of individuals seeking information about possible suspects who might have been seen dressing quickly after the crime, but none were found. Police estimated that as much as six to ten minutes went by before the health club management actually realized what had taken place and authorities were called. Investigators also questioned countless individuals about either members or employees of the club who were known for having violent tempers, as whoever killed Jonathan Pelzer had seemingly drastically overreacted over an apparent oversight regarding grooming manners.

Investigators followed up as to several members who had lost control over one thing or another; however only one had been present at the club at the time of the crime, and he had been working out on the second floor in front of a dozen witnesses at the time of the offense. Similarly, investigators learned that the victim had once made a racial comment in front of a Black club member and had been quickly called on it. However, it was quickly determined that the Black member was out of town at the time of the crime and therefore was eliminated as a suspect. He did say, however, that the victim regularly said nasty things about others, both as to racial and other unkind remarks. All of these investigative inquiries failed to result in any form of sustainable lead, and months later the case remained unsolved.

Starting Over

Typically all homicide investigations should begin with a complete background investigation of the victim. By learning all about one's life it is often possible to identify a person with a motive for the crime. However, little of this had taken place in the Pelzer case due to the certainty on the part of investigators that he had been killed in a spontaneous act of rage over a seeming slight inside a steam room.

Six months into the investigation a new team of investigators were assigned to the case. Like any good cold case investigators, they began as if the crime was an hour old. They soon learned the following:

1) Jonathan and Mimi Pelzer were not especially loyal to one another. Both had a list of indiscretions with others – some single, others married.

2) On one occasion the husband of Jonathan's companion learned of the cheating and had confronted the victim in an expensive restaurant.

3) The victim collected lawsuits as the result of questionable business practices by the dozen.

4) Therefore, he did not lack for enemies, at least one of whom might wish him dead.

Working Leads

Mimi Pelzer admitted to the new investigators that she had sexual relations with several men during the course of her marriage to her husband. She said that she had gone through a period as did many others in her set where too much alcohol and a touch of cocaine led to what she called "recreational sex." She also said that Jonathan had his playthings, something she just never really wanted to know much about. "In our set," she said, "refined adults are afforded a great deal of discretion to carry out their activities just so long that it doesn't become a public issue."

The once irate husband was just as philosophical about the victim having gone to bed with his wife. He had been drinking heavily when the victim walked into the restaurant bar where he was sitting, and so he told Pelzer what a slime he was. But instead of killing him he decided to hit on Mimi, which he did do on several occasions. Mimi later confirmed the suspect's story.

Lastly, business enemies were questioned. All agreed that "business was just that . . . You win some and next time you get outsmarted, but people like us do not kill over it."

By the time the new investigators completed their interviews, all had stated in one way or another that Jonathan Pelzer was a first-rate jerk who was missed by few, but nobody seemed capable of gathering enough passion to take his life.

Assessment of Case Facts

There were two ways to view what the investigators had learned. One was that the victim had been disliked by a wide variety of friends, lovers, and enemies, none of whom happened to have it in them to kill him. The opposite view was that if someone is disliked by enough parties, then at least one of them just might want him dead. In this instance the investigators decided to look closest to home. They gained Mimi's phone records and found an interesting series of calls made from her cell phone to a known Mafia member named Alfie Morano. He was high enough up the chain of command so that he clearly had the capability of arranging for the type of ending that Jonathan Pelzer had met.

---

Investigators returned to the health club in search of a way that hired killers might have gained access to the facility. All members must present their membership card at the front desk, and guests must be with a member and fill out a two-page form before entering the club. They then have their photo taken, which becomes electronically attached to the member's file. It took several hours to go through the photos of everyone who had passed by the membership desk in the 24 hours leading up to the crime. Each photo was compared with a gallery of known crime syndicate members based on the theory that Alfie Morano had set up a hit on the victim on behalf of Mimi, however nothing whatsoever matched.

The investigators then walked back to the men's locker room to take yet another look at what had been the crime scene. They were interrupted by a mentally handicapped attendant whose job it was to pick up wet towels. "Did you catch the guys who did it yet?" he said.

One of the investigators told him that they were still working on it, then asked, "Did you know the man who was killed?"

"Fat slob," the attendant said. "He made a mess and never cleaned up."

The investigators asked the young man to show them just what he saw Jonathan Pelzer do in the locker room. The fellow dramatically went through the motions of dumping his gym bag outside the locker, then moved to the row of sinks where he pretended to be shaving. Then he walked to the steam room, before turning around laughing, obviously proud of his parody.

"So where did the man leave his dirty razor?"

The attendant ran back to the sink and pointed to the counter.

And so this was the start of a really good theory that matched the known facts of the case.

A Theory Advanced

It can be very dangerous business to assume motive based on the location of the homicide. For example, if an individual works in a retail setting, the first thought might be that the motive was robbery. In the Pelzer case the word of witnesses made it seem absolutely certain that the victim had been killed in the course of a senseless act of rage over poor hygiene techniques. However, consider the theory that follows based on known facts of the case.

1) Somebody (Mimi, perhaps) wanted the victim dead.

2) That individual had certain connections with organized crime.

3) The hired killers were told of his habit of visiting the health club.

4) A plan was devised whereby the killers found a way to gain entry into the club (Method yet to be determined).

5) Dressed in workout attire they waited for the victim to return to the locker room.

6) The victim shaved at the sink as the attendant stated, leaving the razor on the counter.

7) The victim entered the steam room. The steam was sufficiently dense so that only shapes of persons could be made out.

8) The two killers sat on either side of the victim, after having picked up the victim's razor.

9) Killer A said to stop shaving in the steam room.

10) Killer B responded with a profane statement as if the words had actually come from the victim.

11) The killers smashed the victim's head against the tile wall in back of where he sat, killing him instantly. They then dropped the victim's razor by his feet to make it seem like he had just used it.

12) They moved quickly out the back way of the men's locker room, then into the door of the family locker room.

13) By walking thirty feet to the front of that locker room they were able to exit only feet away from the lobby and were soon out into the parking lot.

---

The crime may or may not have taken place as theorized, however the actual point is that it could have logically occurred as described. Once they learned from the locker room attendant that the victim had shaved before entering the steam room all else began to fall into place. Few men who shave at a sink and mirror are likely to then do a subsequent close shave in the steam room.

A Mystery Within the Mystery

Where the new investigators were stumped was just how the killers were able to gain entry into the club, past the tight security and computerized check-in system. The reception desk was to the right as one entered the club. To the right of that was the café, and to the immediate left upon entry was the salon.

Once again they spoke to club management. The two questions were whether or not one might either get their hair done or eat in the café as a non-member. The manager said that non-members did patronize the salon but that they would not be allowed into the common areas of the club. The same went for the café.

Investigators interviewed the café staff who had been working on the day of the crime. The questioning centered around whether anyone recalled a pair of men present on the day of the crime. A cashier with a heavy Polish accent thought that she remembered something since the first wave of police had talked to her. A very tan middle-aged guy with balding gray hair ordered an expresso and then took it over toward the lounge area just beyond the reception desk. She had the idea that he was with another fellow she really never saw.

The thing about the guy with the tan was that he walked into the club with a twenty-something blond who looked like a living Barbie Doll. She went directly into the salon and her companion went directly to the café. The girl had been wearing an expensive orange pants suit, and the suntanned guy wore a matching two-piece navy and white sweat suit.

It took an hour for the salon manager to drive to the club on her day off. She recalled the blond. It took only a moment to call up her information. She had called an hour earlier and made an appointment for a wash and dry styling, giving the name Jennifer West. They had no phone listed for her. The manager called the stylist who did her hair. Of course she remembered, if for no other reason than the girl having acted as if she was terrorized about something. She had been shaking the entire time her hair was being worked on. When asked if she was okay, the girl said that she had just seen a former boyfriend in the club who had treated her poorly, thus accounting for her state of mind. Nobody connected to the salon had noticed whether or not she had walked in with anyone, and nobody, including the front desk personnel, recalled either the blond or her companion or companions.

Case Facts Come Together

Therefore, it was only the young woman in the café who had seen what might have been one of the offenders inside the club. However, there are those moments as a criminal investigator when one suddenly "gets it," where all of the swirling issues come together. Based on their new information it became apparent that the blond acted as a diversion for the killers by getting the desk clerk's attention, stating that she had an appointment at the salon. According to club policy she would have been instructed to walk around members waiting to check in and go directly to get her hair done. At the same instant the two men with her might have simply walked past the desk or perhaps they said that they were going to the café.

The next segment of information came from the café cashier who was certain that the blond and suntanned fellow came in together, then went their separate ways. After having gotten his drink he moved to the lounge area where she thought he met a second man with whom he had entered the club.

What was most significant about the two suspects being placed in the lounge area was the fact that the front entrance to the family locker room was only steps away. A ten-second walk through the family locker room and they would have been only seconds away from the men's locker room, ready to commit the crime in question.

Creating Criminal Activity

Through some excellent reasoning and calculation the investigators had arrived at the point where they thought that they knew how the killers had cleverly created a crime that was designed to divert attention away from the actual motive for the crime. They were not only certain that they knew how the crime had been carried out, but that the victim's wife with the help of an organized crime member had orchestrated the crime.

Investigators showed mugshots of just about every known member of the organized crime community, however health club personnel had not been able to identify anyone. Therefore, of the four individuals thought to have been involved, Mimi Pelzer and Alfie Morano were known but the identity of the actual killers was still a mystery.

Criminal investigation is often a matter of style and technique. Given this set of circumstances many investigators would simply confront Mimi Pelzer with the fact that they had evidence that she had solicited organized crime to kill her husband. Many times such direct tactics have proven successful. Many guilty suspects, when confronted with evidence seemingly sufficient to charge and convict, simply come clean and admit their role and guilt.

However, in this case they did not know the identity of either killer nor of their blond decoy. Therefore the decision was made to "shake some trees" to see what might fall to the ground. They paid a visit to Mimi at her penthouse apartment and told her that they had a young blond woman in custody who had told them that the killing was carried out by members of organized crime. Mimi Pelzer was noticeably rattled but the investigators never let on that they noticed. They stayed only long enough to deliver the message, saying that they would be in touch as soon as the case was solved. Mimi stuttered a bit while asking just how soon that might be. "More like hours than days or weeks," had been their reply.

Auto track scanners had been secreted on both Mimi and Alfie Morano's cars, a Bentley and

60

Jaguar respectively, meaning that police surveillance teams could track the paths of the cars from up to a mile away. They also had security tracks on both suspects' cell phones, a task that was made easier by the fact that both of them used the same communication company.

Mimi had called Alfie before the investigators were able to complete the elevator ride down from penthouse to lobby. Alfie in turn made two calls immediately thereafter. He then started up his green Jaguar and drove to a hot dog stand, which was known to be owned by a Mafia member. Standing at the counter waiting for Alfie Morano was a deeply tanned guy wearing a St. Louis Cardinal cap. They spoke for less than a minute; baseball cap left first and drove off in a rental convertible and was followed by a surveillance team involving three cars. Others stayed with Alfie via auto track hidden on the frame of his car.

Alfie then drove to a nearby coffee shop where he met with a big strong looking fellow wearing a cheap toupee'. Alfie left and drove home, while the other guy drove to a nightclub near the airport. Seconds later the rental convertible arrived. If the investigative plan were to be totally successful, the blond decoy would be inside the nightclub.

She was.

A female member of the investigative surveillance team followed the suspects into the bar. The cashier at the health club café had been right on in her description of the blond as looking like a Barbie Doll. Behind the bar she waited on the pair. She told the suntanned suspect to take off his baseball cap as they were not allowed in the club. The investigator sat halfway down the bar from the others and placed a dime-sized recorder near her knee at the base of the bar. The device was able to pick up conversations hundreds of feet away, so fifteen feet would be no problem whatsoever.

The three suspects were engaged in a highly animated conversation that did not need to be overheard in order to understand that she was spending all of her time denying that she had talked to the police or anyone else about the case.

When recording devices and other technology are used in homicide investigations, the police usually take their time to study the nature and extent of their evidence before making any drastic moves; but in this case things would have to take place quicker than that. Once Mimi told Alfie Morano that the blond had talked, he would soon figure out that the investigators had set them all up with the planted false information. Then everyone would clean up and possibly take off.

As the surveillance team listened to the suspects' conversation about having been at the health club, the investigative decision was made to move in on the suspects as their conversation seemed to be concluding. Three minutes later the trio were all handcuffed and on their way to investigative headquarters in separate vehicles. The lead investigators had filmed the arrests depicting the suspects being led to unmarked squad cars handcuffed behind their backs. They then hopped into their own car to rush the film to show Mimi. Before the three suspects arrived at headquarters Alfie Morano was arrested at his home and would soon join the others. Now it was just a matter of who would break first and confess.

Interrogation Issues

Bright investigators attempt to gain a confession in every homicide case. Regardless of the nature of other evidence courts tend to believe it when the police testify that a defendant admitted to the crime. Stated another way, a confession acts to greatly strengthen any court case.

At first glance it might seem as if it is not to the advantage of a criminal suspect to admit his/her guilt to the police. Why would anyone confess if his/her admission all but sealed his/her being found guilty at trial? The answer is based on damage control and survival when possibly faced with a stiff prison sentence or even the death penalty. Simply put, many criminal suspects begin the plea-bargaining process in the interrogation room with the police.

When there are multiple suspects involved in a crime, the state's tactic is often to interrogate the least involved suspect first in the hope that he/she will involve the more involved. In the Pelzer case the police would be most interested in gaining proof against those who actually carried out the crime, then those who arranged the crime, down to those who might have assisted in the crime.

In the Pelzer case the least involved individual was the blond decoy who entered the health club just ahead of the killers, therefore she would be the first to be questioned.

Her name was Holly Hart and she was an aspiring actress. The way the investigators had the case figured was that the baseball cap and toupee' duo were the likely killers actually inside the steam room. Alfie Morano would have arranged the crime on behalf of Mimi Pelzer.

Holly Hart said that she was an aspiring actress from Iowa City, Iowa. She had been a bartender at the club where the investigators found her for two years. She met Alfie Morano across the bar and he asked her if she wanted to spend a half day at a first-rate spa as a tip for her good service. On the morning in question she rode with the same pair who had been in the club when the arrests were made. She knew them only as Julius and Reggie as they never used credit cards in the bar.

It wasn't until the next day that she heard about the murder of Jonathan Pelzer on the ten o'clock news on the bar television. Even then she thought it was a coincidence that a murder had occurred at a place where she had her hair done. The police interrogators quickly moved her past that lie, which led her to admitting that Morano and the others subsequently discussed the crime in front of her at the bar. From that night on whenever any of the three suspects were in the club they always left her at least a hundred-dollar tip. An hour later she gave a taped statement implicating all three of them in the murder. She had heard numerous references to someone named Mimi, but she had no idea who she was or what her part in the crime might have been.

# CASE 2

## RELATIONSHIP AND STRANGER MURDERS

Investigative Overview

Most murder victims are killed by a person they knew in life. Therefore, most murders are solved by (1) conducting a thorough investigation into the victim's life, then (2) identifying a suspect from the victim's life with a motive for the crime. Relationship murders are easier to solve than stranger murders if for no other reason than the actual pool of suspects is finite. By contrast a robbery-murder may have been committee by any of a million persons in a large urban area.

Thus the wisest possible killers might know that by being able to make a relationship killing look otherwise, their chances of getting away with the crime becomes excellent.

# CASE 2

<u>The Crime</u>

　　Julia Maki was a 43-year-old physician who lived in a suburb near a major city with her husband, Robert, and her eight-year-old son, Bobby. Early on a Saturday morning a neighbor saw her pull out of her driveway and head toward a main street where there was a large shopping center. At 11:00 a.m., some three hours later, a shopper looked into Julia's car and saw her spread out and leaning across the front seat. He called the police who quickly determined that she was dead.

　　Crime scene investigators determined that the driver's side door did not open by use of either the inside or outside handle. The victim had swelling and the beginning of discoloration to the front of her neck. She wore cotton slacks, a pullover shirt, athletic socks, and seemingly brand new white tennis shoes. The right sock and top of the shoe was soiled by what might have been grease. Only two sets of fingerprints were lifted from the car. It would later be determined that they belonged to the victim and her son, who regularly rode in the car. The medical examiner's report would state that the cause of death was manual strangulation. No purse or wallet was found inside the car, which did not appear to have been searched through. The key was in the ignition in the "off" position.

　　Police questioned shoppers as they returned to the parking lot near the victim's car. One woman reported that she had seen a "scary looking Black guy" walking nearby in the lot when she exited her car an hour earlier. The police arranged for the woman to help create a composite sketch later in the day.

An investigator went to the victim's house a mile away and made the death notification to the husband who was busy painting the front steps when he arrived. The husband became disoriented when told of the death to the extent that he sat down on a step covered with wet paint. Robert Maki then told the police the following regarding the occurrences on the last morning of Julia Maki's life.

1) He awoke at 7:00 a.m., made coffee, and brought Julia a cup in bed. She told him that she had a headache, got up to take an aspirin, and then went back to sleep.

2) Their son Bobby woke up at about 7:30 a.m., went into the living room and watched cartoons. The dad then got him ready as a cousin would pick Bobby up for a children's birthday party.

3) On his way out the door Bobby went to the bedroom door, said goodbye to Julia, and then left.

4) Robert went to the basement, mixed his paint, and went to work on the steps.

5) At about 8:00 a.m. Julia exited the house through the attached garage, said goodbye, backed her car out of the driveway, and headed toward the shopping center.

6) Robert confirmed that the driver's side door was jammed and would not open.

7) He said that she was a cautious woman who would have been wary of dangerous looking strangers.

Background Investigation of Victim

Julia Maki was a quiet and modest woman who had been a highly rated physician for more than a decade. She had two brothers who were renowned surgeons on the West Coast. She had been married to Robert, an insurance agent, for twelve years. Neighbors said that he screamed at his family on a regular basis, though there was no evidence that he was physically abusive.

Investigators learned that Julia had recently taken out a $250,000 life insurance policy that paid double in the event of a non-natural death. That made Robert suddenly worth a half-million dollars.

Digging for a Motive

The insurance policy had been purchased from an associate of Robert Maki. Robert hand-carried the policy home for Julia to sign, he said, then returned it to the other agent. When compared to the signature on her driver's license, the signature on the policy looked valid; however the crime lab would make the final decision as to that. What was certain was that Robert Maki was the only person capable of stating that he had seen the victim sign the insurance policy. Four monthly payments had been made, each with a money order made out to the insurance company. They had been issued by a currency exchange near the hospital where the victim worked. None of the six currency exchange employees had any notion as to who had bought them. The victim's personal checking account did not reflect checks written on corresponding dates in conjunction with the money order purchases, but that did not mean that she had not purchased them to pay for the policy.

None of the victim's relatives knew anything about the insurance policy, but all agreed with one thing – had Julia taken out such an insurance policy, the beneficiary would have been the son, Bobby, and not Robert.

Investigators searched for a criminal history on Robert Maki and found an arrest under the name Bobby Maki, a name Robert never was known to use. Interestingly, Bobby Maki used the son's day and month of birth and the father's year of birth. Of far greater interest were the circumstances surrounding the arrest. Bobby Maki had been arrested in a downtown hotel room in the company of a 26-year-old woman named Beatriz Buena. It seems that the two were found in bed together in the hotel room, however they had failed to either register at the hotel or pay for the room. Thus they were charged with trespass to property. When investigators spoke to the arresting officers, they were told that the apparent girlfriend was very pregnant. Thus what seemed like a pair of Major League motives for murder had surfaced: $500,000 and a young girlfriend probably pregnant with his child.

Knowing it is one thing, proving it is another.

## Following Leads

At the time the investigators arranged for the witness, who had seen the Black suspect near the victim's car, to help create a composite sketch, they had no idea of the nature of the condemning evidence against Robert Maki. However, the wise investigative decision remained to follow all leads regardless of appearances, therefore the composite sketch was made. Once the sketch was viewed by officers in the station, a pair of tactical officers stated that they thought they knew who the sketch was of. They soon produced a mugshot of a fellow named Arthur Wells, who was a known purse snatcher and strong-armed robber. The witness was then shown a photo gallery and immediately identified Wells as the person that she had seen loitering near the victim's car.

Wells was picked up on a street corner and taken to the station for questioning. There was no way of predicting how the interrogation might go since the suspect was clearly under the influence of some probable combination of alcohol and drugs. The pair of investigators joined the suspect inside the interrogation room and noticed that Wells was sitting at the table at an odd angle with one leg pointed straight out to the side.

"Move your foot, Arthur," said one investigator. "I want to see what you're hiding."

"Hiding, hiding, I'm not hiding nothing," Wells replied.

"Stand up or just pick up whatever is beneath your foot."

The suspect swore and leaned over and then handed a credit card over to the police. It was Julia Maki's Visa Card.

"I took it from the lady but she was already dead, and that's the truth," said Wells.

---

In some homicide investigations a suspect never surfaces. Now the police had a pair of prime suspects – a husband who had every reason to wish his wife dead, and a robber in possession of the victim's credit card.

Arthur Wells told the following story: He needed to finance his heroin habit and was therefore up early. He walked to the shopping center and walked around looking for a car with an open window in order to commit a theft. Arthur said that he arrived there just before 9:00 a.m. and it was not long after that that he saw the victim behind the wheel of her car. He watched for a minute waiting for her to get out of the car since he noticed that the passenger-side window was open. However, she never got out of the car, so he walked around the other end of the lot looking for something to rip off. Maybe fifteen or twenty minutes later he went back to the area where the victim was parked and to his surprise she was still sitting behind the wheel. He then figured that she was either asleep or drunk and as he neared he could see that she was slumped over and definitely not moving. He walked up to the passenger side and saw her purse on the seat alongside the victim.

He reached in and grabbed the purse, stuffed it inside his sweatshirt, and headed toward the nearest alley. Julia's wallet had four twenty-dollar bills in it and a pair of credit cards, the one he just got caught with and another he traded for two bags of heroin.

The suspect asked just why it was that the police were working so hard on a simple purse theft. When told that it was a homicide investigation, the suspect suddenly became a whole lot less high. Arthur stiffened up and became bug-eyed.

"You mean that lady was dead," he said.

"Did you make her that way, Arthur?"

"I watched that lady for a half hour before I grabbed her purse and she never once moved. If she's dead she was just as dead the first time I saw her," he said. "I'll show you where I tossed the purse. It's in a dumpster by the KFC.

"And if she's dead, I tell you one more thing. The dude who did it shoots pool," said Arthur. "Her purse had blue chalk on it."

Arthur Wells was right on with his information. The purse was right where he said it would be, and it did have the same kind of blue chalk pool players use on their cues. However, the robber turned detective did miss one other clue; the purse also had a spot on it that had the same black grease as was found on the victim's sock and tennis shoe.

## Medical Examiner's Report Analyzed

Somebody used their hands to strangle Julia Maki. Seemingly the killer placed both thumbs across the front of the throat. This would indicate that the killer and victim were facing one another at the time of the attack. Applied to the case conditions, the victim could not have been killed by someone who approached her as she sat behind the steering wheel. Had the killer reached through the open driver's side window his thumbs would have been placed at the back of the victim's neck with the fingers centered on the front of her neck. Other avenues of entry into the car would have been greatly limited by the fact that the driver's door would not open. The only manner by which the crime could have been carried out would have been for the killer to enter the passenger's side door, sit on the right bucket seat, then lean over and grab the victim while facing her.

Markings on the neck indicated that the killer's hands were small enough for the act to have been committed by a woman. The time of death was estimated to have been between 7:00 and 11:00 a.m. A police canvass resulted in two neighbors agreeing that they had seen the victim drive past their houses at just about 8:00 a.m. To the extent that their information was correct, the victim would have arrived alive at the shopping center at about 8:10 a.m. Arthur Wells said that the victim was motionless inside her car at just about 9:00 a.m. shortly after his arrival at the parking lot.

## Measuring Suspects

That Arthur Wells may have been the killer was not difficult to imagine as he had a criminal history that included two robberies of female victims so he was clearly not adverse to the potential of acting out violence upon women. In this instance Wells either stole from a dead woman or he made her dead. Wells' bond was set at $500,000 on a theft charge, so he would not be going anywhere soon. Thus the investigators had no problem visiting him in jail for two separate reasons. First, they wanted to see if his account of the facts remained consistent; and second, they wanted to take a good look at his hands.

At the time of his initial arrest they searched his hands and nails for physical evidence, but at the time they had no idea that they were seeking a killer with small hands. No such luck. Wells told the same story and his hands were large enough to have easily palmed a basketball.

Investigators then knocked on Robert Maki's front door, which had a brand new coat of paint on it from the murder day. He answered the door and shook the hand of an investigator who offered his condolences. His soft right hand was the size of a Campfire Girl's. Before the investigator could ask to come inside to speak to him, Robert handed them a business card with the name of his newly retained attorney. In the words of the authorities, Robert Maki had "lawyered up," most surprisingly prior to his having been accused of anything.

In the eyes of the police only those with things to hide invoke their Miranda rights and refuse to talk to the police. In this instance it seemed as if Robert Maki called great suspicion to himself at a time when he really didn't need to do that. Thus the sides had been chosen; the widower had said, "Prove I did it." While the police said, "Knowing it is one thing, proving it is another."

How it Was Done

If the killer was Arthur Wells, there is no great mystery about the inner workings of the crime. He would have spotted the victim as she pulled up in her car, jumped in and strangled her while facing her as she was behind the wheel. However, there are two problems with that possibility: The first is that Wells is big and strong enough to have easily overpowered Julia Maki in taking her purse, thus there would have been no apparent reason to have killed her. The second problem with Wells as the killer is that a witness would have been likely to have seen him in the act of the crime; recall that one witness did see him lurking about in the parking lot.

If Robert Maki was behind the crime, the question becomes just how the crime might have been carried out. In such an instance there are two huge problems: The victim was said to have been seen driving away from the house very much alive, and Robert was seen by neighbors painting his front steps at the apparent time of the crime. To the extent that both statements are accurate, Robert Maki could not possibly have personally killed his wife, rather he would have had to have solicited someone else to carry out the crime.

One of the keys to successful criminal investigation is the ability to create a framework of events that adequately accounts for all known facts of the case. Both the victim and her surviving husband were of Filipino extraction. The lady who stated that she saw Julia drive by was elderly and might have been subject to the type of common assumptions that often cloud investigations. Certainly, the witness must have seen the victim's car leave the Maki driveway and cruise past her house. Having recognized the victim's car she might have simply taken for granted that it had actually been the victim driving. Perhaps she might have even looked at the car carefully as it passed her house. The question then becomes, would she have noticed had the car been driven by a different Asian woman, such as Robert Maki's pregnant girlfriend? The answer is probably not.

The next question becomes, why Robert Maki might have had his girlfriend drive the victim's car from the family house to the shopping center. The girlfriend could not have possibly transported a dead woman inside the car to the parking lot. In the first place a lone pregnant woman could not have handled the victim's dead weight to move her from one point inside the car to behind the steering wheel. Moreover, the fact that the driver's side door of the victim's car did not open, thus making the job all the more difficult.

The four-hour window of the victim's death does leave room for the husband to have strangled her inside the family home. If the plan was to make it appear that the killing occurred in the parking lot, the girlfriend might have had the job of driving slowly down the block upon leaving the residence, hoping that she would both be seen and mistaken for the victim, which of course did happen.

The theory thus takes on the killing having taken place at home and the victim's car having been transported to where she was found. The next element becomes a matter of just how the victim's body was moved from Point A to Point B. Obviously at least a second accomplice would have had to have been involved whose role it would have been to transport the body to meet the arrival of the victim's car at the parking lot.

Analyzing Evidence

The physical evidence submitted to the crime lab included

1) White canvas shoes with a grease mark.
2) White cotton sock with a grease mark.
3) Purple cloth purse with blue stain near clasp.

---

Items 1 and 2 were found to be a general grease/oil lubricant commonly used to free sticking parts. Item 3 was precisely what Arthur Wells had said it was, blue billiard chalk.

Logic and reasoning is such that it is more likely than not that the victim's clothing and apparel came in contact with both substances in the course of one common event as opposed to separate from one another. Given that the killer's task at hand was to transport the victim's dead remains from her home to where she was found, the most reasonable notion would be that she came in contact with the grease and billiard chalk while inside the trunk of an auto.

The investigative question then became how to actually go about placing investigative leads to work toward solving the crime. The two pieces of physical evidence would eventually come together if the case were to be cleared. For example, the automotive grease lead might move investigators toward the billiard chalk lead, but those particular odds were very long indeed. Chances were actually much better that the chalk would lead to a suspected accomplice that would then lead investigators to the sought-after car.

Within twenty miles of the crime scene there were over two dozen pool halls plus a few thousand taverns with pool tables. Thus, the need was to take the general lead dealing with the billiard chalk and attempt to make it far more specific. Investigators considered that Julia and Robert Maki were both Filipino as was his pregnant girlfriend who they now suspected of having driven the victim's car on the morning of the crime. Therefore it would not be at all a stretch to think that perhaps the other accomplice was also Filipino as well.

Investigators soon learned that pocket billiards is quite popular with Filipinos and that one particular parlor in the nearby major city was populated nearly entirely by them. Before setting out to that billiard parlor the investigators met with the crime lab technician who identified the physical evidence. She explained that billiard chalk is used to match the color of the table's cloth. More than 90% of all tables – including nearly all bar tables – have green cloth. Therefore, find a place with blue tables and chances are excellent that the accomplice might be connected to such a place. The technician also said that her best guess was that the grease on the victim's sock and shoe came from the inside of an auto with a sticky trunk lock. Thus the investigators would be looking for a suspect frequently at a pool hall with blue tables and would be driving an older auto with a trunk look that needed lubrication.

Investigative Legwork

Between dusk and the following early morning the investigators staked out a certain pool hall with blue tables that was populated by many Asian players, some of whom were seemingly Filipino. They watched people arrive and leave and noted the license number and description of their auto. After catching a few hours of sleep they would begin running the plates for registration information, then take the owners' name and run those for criminal histories. Usually when folks help move dead bodies they have come to the attention of the police in the past.

It was nearly dawn when the investigators made their way toward home from the major city.

As they exited from the highway, they stopped to buy a morning newspaper from a vendor standing along the yellow line. They were nearly back at their station house when the passenger told the driver to turn around. "Go back to the newspaper guy. If the guy we're looking for started early and if he also came from the city, he probably went back and forth past our exit. Therefore he might have also been seen by the vendor." So they decided to ask him.

"Were you out here Saturday morning at this time?"

"I'm here every morning, long about 4:00 a.m. 'til nearly noon. Some days I sell three hundred papers."

"You didn't happen to see a Filipino guy westbound before daybreak or back on his way home maybe seven or so, did you?"

"You must subscribe to Dion Warwick's Psychic Hotline. Big mean looking dude with greasy curls. He looks just as much Black as Filipino, like he's probably a war baby," the vendor said.

"What was he driving?" asked the investigator.

"Big old white Cadillac Seville with a gold-colored grille. Maybe ten years old or so. Car had no plates, just the cardboard applied for."

And that's how murders sometimes get solved.

The suspect the newspaper vendor had described had been out in front of the pool hall with blue tables populated by Asians talking with a group of individuals. Just as the vendor said, he was something of a sinister looking guy. The investigators did not see him arrive and he left with a group of people in a red Audi, therefore there was no way at this point to identify him, and the white Cadillac he had driven had been nowhere in sight.

Investigative Choice

The billiard parlor would be reopening in only a few hours in the morning, so the investigators might just go there and talk to the manager to learn their suspect's name. In that way they might have him identified in short order. However, the downside to that plan might be that the manager would deny knowing the suspect, then notify him of the police interest in him. If so, both the suspect and the white Cadillac would be gone. Thus it became an easy choice; the investigators would grab some sleep and then head back to set up another surveillance to wait for a large suspect with greasy curls.

Hours later the investigators were back in place. Not long after, the white Cadillac pulled to the curb directly in front of the billiard parlor. The driver got out and was exactly as described. He had shiny black curls, high cheek bones, a pock-marked face, and was tall and wiry. The investigators ran his license plate that registered to a Steve Alteri at an address only blocks away from the billiard parlor.

The investigators ran his criminal history sheet and learned that he had done time for a battery offense in which he struck his victim with, of all things, a pool cue. While in prison he had another two years added to the sentence for another battery upon an inmate. He had been out on the streets for a year.

## Working With the Law

In terms of actual legal evidence the investigators had nothing on Steve Alteri. Nobody placed him at the victim's home, and as far as the police knew nobody saw him at the parking lot where the victim was to be found. All they had was that there had been blue billiard chalk on the victim's purse and that a guy in a white Cadillac had driven to and from their city to not far from the crime scene. Though the suspect fit the crime as an accomplice, the police did not have enough evidence to get a warrant to seize and search Alteri's Cadillac.

However, that was not to be required. Alteri got into the Cadillac, drove away from the billiard parlor, and quickly was speeding twenty miles over the limit. The investigators turned on their siren and pulled him over.

"Step out of the car, friend."

"That badge says you're not even the police in this city," Alteri said.

"We're sworn by the State. Step out of the car and show me your license and insurance card."

While one investigator talked to the suspect, the other checked the inside of the car. A .25 caliber automatic was found beneath the front seat armrest. Steve Alteri was under arrest, and the arrest gave the investigators the legal right to tow and impound the Cadillac.

The Interrogation

Contrary to popular belief most interrogation interactions between the police and suspects are not hostile. The police must logically go about explaining to the suspect the facts of the case and the specific ways in which the suspect is linked to the crime. In the Maki case Steve Alteri was told the truth as to the following case facts.

1) Julia Maki was killed in her own house and her body transported to a shopping center parking lot.

2) That blue billiard chalk was found on her purse.

3) That grease from a trunk lock was found on her shoe and sock.

4) That once the crime lab finds the same kind of chalk and grease in the Cadillac's trunk, the State will prove that the victim's dead body was transported in your trunk.

5) The State has a witness that saw you driving the car from and to the city on the morning that the incident occurred.

---

Steve Alteri nodded his head stating, "The old man selling newspapers . . . I worried about that." Thus the investigators had their incriminating statement. All of the rest was to follow:

Robert Maki did take out the insurance policy on the victim and forged her name on it. He then made payments through money orders from an unknown currency exchange. On the overnight in question Robert Maki strangled his wife in their bed. When the son went to the bedroom to say goodbye to his mother, the sheet covered all but her hair; and the boy simply assumed that she was sleeping. In reality, it had been the girlfriend in his mother's bed.

As the police knew from the newspaper vendor, Alteri drove from the city to get the victim's body from inside the attached garage before daybreak. What the police had not known, however, was that Alteri had also driven the girlfriend in the Cadillac as well. She had stayed on the floor of the backseat.

Upon arrival at the Maki house Robert opened the garage door, Steve backed the car inside, the girlfriend got out of the car, and Julia was placed in the trunk of the car. Unfortunately, Alteri dropped the body onto a pool cue case he had left inside the trunk and some of the blue chalk rubbed off onto her purse. He then drove to an all-night diner and waited for the girlfriend to drive the victim's car to the lot where Alteri drove up, popped the trunk, and moved the body that was covered by a wool blanket. The girlfriend jumped from the victim's car and got into the back of the Cadillac. Alteri took the blanket, tossed it into the car, and they were gone.

An investigator asked whether he was concerned about placing a dead body inside the car, but Alteri said that the stores were at least thirty minutes from opening and there were no cars within the length of a football field.

The investigators recovered the blanket Alteri told them about, and the crime lab was able to conclusively place the victim inside the trunk of the Cadillac. Based on Steve Alteri's statement the investigators were able to obtain a search warrant for the Maki family house. There they found evidence that proved everything had happened just as stated: Julia had been killed in her own bed, moved to the garage, kept there until transported by Alteri, then dumped in her own car.

Robert Maki and Beatriz Buena were tried and found guilty of the murder of Julia Maki. Steve Alteri entered a plea to a lesser charge and testified against the others. This leaves just one last issue, that being, how did Robert Maki and Steve Alteri know one another? The answer is that Maki was Alteri's auto insurance agent, and one day over policy renewal talk they also settled on another business matter that was supposed to make Alteri $25,000 richer once Julia's insurance policy was paid off.

# CASE 3

## RIGHT THEORY, WRONG SUSPECT

Investigative Overview

A man was shot in the doorway to his house by someone who had knocked on the door. Soon after the police received an anonymous message stating that the killing was the result of a family feud. The police were given the alleged name of the killer, along with various pieces of information about the killer's relationship and lifestyle.

Investigators quickly located the apparent killer, however nothing they did in their investigation got them any closer to proving their case. They did understand the motive for the crime, and also knew the killer's place in all this.

But the police investigators had identified the wrong actual suspect. After having spent several hundred hours attempting to prove their case, the investigators were going to be forced to start over.

# CASE 3

## The Crime

Jeff Stone was with his girlfriend and their infant son on the living room floor watching television just before midnight. It was a week before Christmas and the weather outside was nearly blizzard-like. The outside door to their two-flat was unlocked and soon there was a knock at their first-floor door. A voice from the hallway said, "Is that you, Jeff?" The victim cracked the door open while his girlfriend remained on the floor half asleep next to the child. Suddenly there were two loud reports from a handgun and the victim fell to the floor, shot once each in the right cheek and the center of his forehead. The victim was quickly transported to a nearby hospital but never regained consciousness and died before being able to describe his killer.

## The Crime Scene

The door to the apartment opened from the right as the killer looked at the victim. One .45 caliber slug traveled through the victim and to the right into the living room, bouncing off of fireplace bricks before landing on the living room floor. The other round struck the wall to the right of the fireplace and was lodged in the plaster about sixty-six inches above the floor. Both slugs traveled within three feet of where the girlfriend and child rested on the floor.

The girlfriend told investigators about the knock at the door and the offender calling to the victim. She was far too stunned to have paid attention to the offender leaving the building, and his voice was not familiar to her, nor was there anything distinctive about either his voice or pattern of speech. She explained that Jeff had returned home about an hour before from his usual Thursday bowling night with friends from work. There was nothing unusual about his behavior, indicating that he was seemingly not in trouble with anyone.

Background Check of Victim

The victim had no criminal history, seldom drank to intoxication, did not use street drugs, and generally got along well enough with most people. The notable exception to that fact was his relationship with the girlfriend. They frequently quarreled that led to the couple being both verbally and sometimes physically abusive to one another. Interestingly, the girlfriend was matter-of-fact about the problems attached to their domestic life. Similarly, Jeff's friends attached little importance about their fights. Both of them seemingly accepted the nature of their fights as being more or less normal despite the fact that she would occasionally call her parents to come and remove her and all three kids when fights were worse than usual.

As to motive for the crime, both the girlfriend and Jeff's friends agreed that they could not imagine any reason for what appeared to be an execution-style murder.

Early Investigation

Next the investigators spoke to the victim's family who uniformly stated that they felt that the girlfriend's family was in some way involved in the crime. However, none of the opinions included anything in the way of tangible evidence to support their theory. Nor did any of the girlfriend's immediate family have a criminal history.

Two days later the police got a break in the case when they received an anonymous phone call from a woman in the town of Westerville, some twenty miles from where the crime took place. She stated the following:

1)  The killer's name was Jose Sosa.
2)  Sosa had recently been paroled from prison after serving a sentence for murder.
3)  Sosa was from a certain neighborhood in a nearby major city.
4)  He was an adult leader of the Latin Souls street gang.
5)  He frequented a certain street corner in the town where the crime took place.
6)  Sosa drove a gray Cadillac.
7)  He had been paid a large amount of money by a member of the girlfriend's family to commit the murder.
8)  The caller did know the victim's girlfriend.

———————————

The police department was able to trace the call to a pay phone in Westerville but was not able to identify the caller. Investigators searched police and prison release information and located a Jose Sosa who at one time had lived in Westerville. They quickly assumed that this Sosa was the individual the caller had made reference to. Once his police file was examined it was determined that much of what the caller had stated fit the suspect, at least in a general way.

1) He had just been released from prison for attempted murder.
2) Sosa was a leader of the Latin Rouser gang, which was affiliated with the Latin Souls.
3) He did have ties to the town where the crime had taken place.
4) He had also been arrested in the major city in question.

Based on Sosa's apparent fit as the subject described by the phone caller, the investigators were able to subpoena their suspect's phone records, the results of which served to further condemn him as the targeted suspect. In the two hours immediately prior to the murder two calls were made from the suspect's phone to two different residences within three blocks of the victim's apartment. Based on this new information the police investigators clearly assumed that the killer had called an accomplice in preparation for carrying out the murder.

Key Investigative Decisions

Investigators decided against confronting anyone connected to the case until they might be able to gather more information, meaning that they did not pick up either Sosa or the girlfriend's family for questioning, nor did they approach the residents of the homes to whom the phone calls had been made on the night of the crime. Instead, they attempted to gather more information on Sosa and the suspected family members. Not surprisingly, after three full months of working the case full time, the investigation was stuck.

Investigative Solution

The case had become stuck largely because the investigators made the decision that they did not want to take actions that would alarm the suspect, meaning both the alleged shooter and the girlfriend's family who had allegedly solicited the commission of the crime. The problem was that the investigators had done just about all they could without alerting the targets of their suspicions. As such, the dynamics were not about to change until new investigative action was taken.

At that juncture another investigator joined the team and talked them into visiting the households to whom the phone calls had been made from Sosa's house. The family at the first residence stated that their daughter was engaged to Sosa's younger brother and called her into the room to speak to investigators. She was very pregnant and willingly said that on the night in question she had been with her boyfriend at the Sosa apartment where everyone was watching football on television. She was bored and called home to talk to her mother. Moments later she made another call to her best friend who lived at the second address only a short distance from the crime scene. That girl was contacted and quickly confirmed that her friend had called her from the Sosa residence.

Investigative Analysis

Up until the investigators' visit to the young woman who made the phone calls, they thought that they had two strong links to Jose Sosa as their targeted suspect – the phone call identifying him as the killer and the phone calls to locations near the victim's house just before the crime. However, the phone calls had been explained away, and the investigators now only had the information from their anonymous source that Jose Sosa was the actual killer.

Searching for Missing Parts

Over the next several days numerous efforts were made to link Sosa to the various pieces of information given them by the anonymous caller: his gang involvement, the place where he once lived, his link to a gray Cadillac, and the local street corner he was alleged to frequent. Police gang and tactical officers were shown the suspect's photo, but none of them knew him. If he was as infamous as described, they should have known who he was. Similarly, there were no links to his supposed major city roots or to the car.

Starting Over

The newest investigator then spoke to his partners regarding his objective view of the situation, which was that absolutely nothing the investigation had disclosed incriminated the targeted suspect, Jose Sosa. As one might imagine the investigator's suggestion that the entire case needed to be started over in search of the actual killer was not well accepted.

However, it was pointed out that when absolutely nothing comes together in an investigation it is usually because of an earlier investigative error or faulty assumption. In this instance it had been reasonable to believe that they had the right suspect, however each fact about him was just slightly different from what the anonymous caller had said about him. The targeted suspect had been in prison for attempted murder, not murder. He was in a different faction of a street gang than was reported by the caller. And there was no link to the street corner or car in question.

The other investigators were reluctant to accept that they had been trailing the wrong person for over three months. "But what about the caller?" they asked. "Are you saying that she was wrong?"

The answer was that the caller was probably right on target, however whoever had searched for Jose Sosa settled on the wrong individual. In reality, it seemed as if he must have been the person the caller was talking about. Not only did most facts fit in a general way, but Sosa had also once lived in the same town where the anonymous call came from.

A New Start

It took less than an hour of digging into data systems to find another Jose Sosa, who upon examination was exactly what the anonymous caller had said he was. He had done prison time for murder, was a member of the correct street gang, had an old address in exactly the area where his roots were said to have been, and the clincher was that this Sosa had been issued a traffic violation in the town where Jeff Stone had been killed. He had been driving a gray Cadillac when stopped by the police, and best yet, the car was registered to Jeff Stone's girlfriend's father.

Thus a relationship between the probable shooter and the people who had hired him for the crime had been established during one morning after nothing had come together in the original investigation over a period of months. Once the correct suspect is identified, criminal investigation suddenly becomes a far easier task.

Things Come Together

Not long after the investigators located the correct Jose Sosa they made certain attempts at interrogating members of his family as to the suspect's involvement in the crime. However nobody was willing to talk. Then a short time later Sosa's long-time girlfriend showed up at a nearby hospital emergency room, the victim of a serious beating. She identified Jose Sosa as being her attacker and immediately became willing to tell about his involvement in the execution murder.

It had been her adult daughter who had made the anonymous call to the police. She made the call out of concern for the family's well-being as Sosa was known for his rage and violence. The crime came about as follows.

After another instance when Jeff Stone's girlfriend called her parents to come over during one of their abusive encounters, Jeff called the mother a vile name. Soon after, the mother went to a pottery class in the community and told the other students about what had happened and how much she wished that Stone were dead. One of the students was Jose Sosa's girlfriend, who stated that if the mother was serious, such a killing might be arranged. Ultimately the deal was consummated whereby the girlfriend's mother paid Sosa $8,000 to kill Jeff Stone.

The mother provided Sosa with the information that Stone went bowling on Thursday nights. The initial plan was for Sosa to shoot him as he got out of his car in front of the apartment, however the victim arrived home earlier than usual before the hitman's arrival. Therefore, he improvised and simply went inside, knocked on the door, and asked if the victim was there. When the victim opened the door, Sosa shot twice as described.

### The Aftermath

The girlfriend's mother was arrested and interrogated. She admitted having solicited the crime through her friend at the pottery class. The mother stated that her daughter knew nothing of the crime, a statement the investigators were certain was true. Had the girlfriend known that the killing was going to take place that night, it is certain that she and her child would not have been present nearby and thus in physical jeopardy.

Jose Sosa was arrested and refused to speak to the investigators. The girlfriend's mother entered a plea of guilty and testified against Sosa at trial. He was found guilty and was sentenced to life in prison. The solicitor was sentenced to eight years for her part in the crime.

Case Summary

At the outset of an investigation there are often several leads that need to be followed. Nearly all leads travel in different paths. All should be followed regardless of the investigator's personal opinion. It should never be said, "I know it didn't happen that way." Each different lead must be worked to its conclusion, which ultimately eliminates that theory or condemns a suspect.

In the Jeff Stone case the investigator who located the initial suspect named Jose Sosa correctly saw that the individual he was looking at seemed to fit the anonymous caller's description in a number of ways. Many times information sources have information that is quite general in nature. Thus they might have heard that the suspect had served time for murder when in reality the charge may have been attempted murder, and so on.

The investigators therefore had every reason to feel certain that they were concentrating on the guilty party. However, after months of searching, absolutely nothing had come together in terms of linking their suspect to the crime except for the two phone calls made from his residence just before the crime. Had the police not waited so long to talk to the young woman who turned out to be going with the suspect's brother, they might have solved the crime far sooner. Once the phone calls no longer linked the suspect to the crime, the investigators had absolutely nothing in the way of tangible evidence linking him to the crime.

It is only because the investigators saw the need to start over that the case was ever solved. Had they stubbornly clung to their initial suspect, the case would have remained stuck. It is in precisely this way that bad investigative outcomes occur; either the case is never solved, or in certain instances the wrong individual is charged with a crime he/she did not commit.

# CASE 4

## OVERCOMING EARLY
## INVESTIGATIVE ERRORS

<u>Investigative Overview</u>

A young woman was stabbed to death in a train station. As one might imagine, the case attracted a great deal of media attention. A composite sketch of the wanted suspect was seen everywhere, yet the case was not solved. Many years later a second victim who survived the attack explained that the sketch artist had actually ignored the description of the killer and drew a sketch of a very different looking individual. Thus it is not surprising that the case went unsolved.

The importance of a good investigative start cannot be overstated. The notable television production, "The First 48," is based on the proposition that if investigators do not come upon an investigative lead in the forty-eight hours immediately following the murder, their chances of eventual case solution is reduced in half.

# CASE 4

A Crime Pattern Analyzed

Bright criminal investigators look for similarities in offenses considering the possibility that one offender or a group of offenders are responsible for similar offenses. Investigators study such elements as offenders' physical description, location and time of day of offenses, and method of operation.

Understanding the probability that an offender is responsible for multiple offenses allows investigators to focus their collective attention on their search and also to predict when the next offense may occur. For example, if an armed robber has committed an offense in each of the past three Tuesdays, chances are excellent that another crime will occur on the upcoming Tuesday. Similarly, by outlining the geographic boundaries of the past crimes, it is possible to predict the general area of the next offense. To the extent that investigators are successful in these various tasks, they create the opportunity to be present and catch the offender in the act of another crime. In less technical past eras crime analysis patterns were done by hand with street maps and stick pins. In this generation all such data is computer generated.

*Incident I – An Attack in the Train Station*

Margaret Wiles was a first-year law student and was waiting to take a train from her suburban home to travel to the university library to study for finals. At 8:00 a.m. on a Saturday she entered the train station and was confronted by a man with a knife. Moments later a middle-aged man named Norman Nelson walked through the turnstile and into the station. He quickly saw that Margaret was naked from the waist down alongside the offender. The attacker whirled around and plunged his knife into the man several times, leaving him for dead. Margaret Wiles seized the opportunity to run up the ramp toward the train platform to get help. However, the offender caught her along the way and stabbed her repeatedly. She died soon after.

Norman Nelson was mortally injured but would survive his injuries. Less than two days after the incident police investigators arrived at the hospital with a graphic artist so that they might generate a composite sketch of the killer. As the artist asked Nelson to describe the offender's facial features, the victim noted that the artist's sketch was not in response to what he was being told. Years later Norman Nelson would state that he was busy describing a clean-cut-looking college student, while the artist was drawing a sinister-looking older fellow with a thin mustache. When Nelson asked why they were not drawing the individual he was describing, he was told that they had their own information.

*Negative Turning-Point I*

By the next day millions of individuals had seen the flyers depicting a suspect that according to the surviving victim looked nothing like the actual offender.

106

*Incident II*

On the morning after Margaret Wiles was murdered and Norman Nelson was stabbed and left for dead, another young woman named Betsy Cooper was sunning herself in a forest preserve area only a mile away from the train station when approached by a clean-cut-looking fellow who looked like a college student. He produced a knife and told her to take her clothes off so that he would not have to kill her. She submitted to the rape and would later tell the police that her attacker was intelligent and well-spoken. She described the offender as follows:

Unknown male, Black, age 19-20, 145-160 pounds, medium complexion, smooth features, clean-shaven.

---

Analysis

The question is thus asked whether it is possible or even likely that the two incidents might have been connected. Consider the following:

1) In both cases the attacker was armed with a knife.

2) Both offenses happened during morning hours.

3) In *Incident I* the surviving victim stated that Margaret Wiles was naked from the waist down. In *Incident II* the victim was instructed to take her clothes off.

4) Both offenses were carried out by a lone offender.

107

5) The two incidents occurred only a mile away from one another.

6) The offender in the Cooper sexual attack fit the description of the actual offender as later described by Norman Nelson.

The above list would indicate that the same offender may have committed both offenses, however such considerations were lost on the investigators due to the fact that they created a composite sketch of an individual that Nelson said was totally inaccurate.

Of primary significance is the fact that the killer's obvious motive was to sexually attack Margaret Wiles. However, once Norman Nelson walked into the train station everything went wrong from the killer's perspective. By having to attack the pair, his need to rape went unsatisfied. Within this context it is most logical that whatever drove him to sexually attack on the first occasion would have remained unsatisfied on the following day. Thus it is logical to believe that he would have sought out another victim as soon as possible.

Had the investigators listened to Norman Nelson, who logically might have been better able to describe his attacker than anyone else, they might have later considered the possibility that they actually had the beginning of a crime pattern on their hands.

---

During the course of that summer there were an even dozen rapes along a jogging path located not far from the forest preserve where Betsy Cooper had been attacked. In each crime the method of operation was essentially the same:

1) A clean-cut-looking young Black man moved toward a woman who was either walking or resting along the jogging path.
2) As he approached, the attacker would smile and make a general observation about nice weather or another equally non-threatening comment.
3) Once within arm's reach of the victim he would produce a knife and force the victim into brush-covered areas along the jogging path.
4) He would then order the victim to disrobe and submit to sexual attack.
5) The attacker was described as bright and well-spoken like a pleasant college student.
6) The physical descriptions supplied by the victims were essentially the same as in the Betsy Cooper offense.

The dozen Jogger Rapes occurred in three different jurisdictions along the path. Only one offense took place in the same town as the Wiles homicide and Cooper rape. Unlike the Wiles investigators, there was no doubt in the minds of the other investigators that they were dealing with a serial rapist. A task force investigative team was formed, but the offenses stopped as autumn arrived and the crime pattern was never solved.

There were no similar offenses over the Midwestern winter months. Then the following May there were three rapes in a new area of the town where Margaret Wiles had been killed. The victims had the same things to say about the attacker: bright, clean-cut in appearance, however he was now described as being slightly larger and more mature looking, for after all it was a year later.

---

A Lead or Not a Lead

Nearly two years after the Wiles homicide patrol officers were sent to a call of an arson incident several blocks from the train station where Wiles had been killed. The caller to the police was a woman who stated that her former boyfriend had just been released from prison after having served a year on an assault case. When she told him that he was not welcome at her house, he left in a rage, only to return a short time later with a can of gasoline that he poured on her front porch and ignited.

By the time the police arrived the suspect had left. However, there was far more to the story. The woman explained that on the morning that Margaret Wiles had been killed her boyfriend had left the house early. Upon his return a couple hours later he was covered with sweat and had bloodstains on his clothing.

Either this was a huge coincidence – something no good investigator believes in – or the police had been handed their killer. The patrol officers called the lead investigator who responded to the scene of the arson, but he quickly told the patrol officers that he knew that the boyfriend was not the killer. The information source was never even spoken to by the investigator.

This story was recounted by one of the patrol officers to a cold case investigator some twenty-five years after the incident. By then the retired sergeant did not recall the location of the arson nor the names of either the information source or that of the suspect she named.

Cold case investigators searched for newspaper records of an arson incident in the area and also conducted a canvass of residents in the area. Nobody knew anything about an arson a quarter of a century earlier.

Prison release records for the year in question were reviewed in search of someone paroled to an address anywhere near the train station. However none of these efforts to identify the suspect were successful.

———————————

There were no similar sex offenses in the area over the winter and spring months. Then in early June there were a pair of rapes on the public way in an area about a mile north of the train station where Margaret Wiles had been killed just over a year before. Once again the offender clearly seemed to be one and the same in both instances: college age, clean-cut, and well-spoken.

Members of the community began to demand answers of the police. What was being done about the ongoing problem of rapes on the public way?

The chief responded by stating that there was no real problem; they were simply experiencing the same amount of rapes present in any town of that size. And most importantly, the crimes were random in nature and not the work of a serial offender.

There were no apparent rapes committed by the handsome, young offender in the next year, then about one a month over the next four summers. With each passing year the offender's description changed and yet remained totally constant. By the sixth year he was described as five to six years older than he was at the beginning of the crime pattern. Similarly, he had matured and gained ten to fifteen pounds, however he was still the same bright, personable rapist.

Then on a stifling hot evening in August Catherine Cappos left her apartment only a block from where three rapes had taken place the previous autumn. She jogged a block, then walked for a while before starting the cycle over again. A witness sitting on his front porch watched Catherine jog by a clean-cut-looking Black man dressed in running attire. As she passed him, he immediately ran after her. Seconds later the witness and numerous others heard screams from an alley directly next to where Catherine had last been seen jogging.

She was found stabbed to death with her running shorts pulled down around her ankles. Police once again generated a composite sketch of the killer. He was a handsome, clean-cut-looking fellow, just like Norman Nelson had described six years earlier. In between the two murders there had been just about 35 rapes, all with the same offender description and method of operation. Ironically enough, the patrol officers in charge of the Catherine Cappos preliminary investigation told reporters that the description of the killer was seemingly identical to that of the offender wanted for three rapes from the past autumn. This was to be the first and only occasion when a member of the police department acknowledged that a serial offender was at large.

Looking Backwards

The order of events as presented is that Margaret Wiles was stabbed to death in an obvious sex-motivated offense. Another woman was raped in a nearby forest preserve the following day. Over the succeeding six years approximately 35 others were sexually attacked within a small geographic area near the murder. Finally, Catherine Cappos was murdered in the vicinity of the prior rapes.

It is to be noted that Norman Nelson recounted the investigative error regarding the killer's depiction in the police composite sketch to a cold case investigator a quarter-century after the offense. At the time that the invalid sketch was generated by the police, nobody asked him whether the sketch actually looked like the killer. Therefore only the two investigators and a sketch artist knew that he said that the depiction of the offender looked nothing like the actual killer. As such, the rest of the outside world – including other police officers and investigators – would have logically assumed they were rightfully seeking the sinister-looking killer in the composite sketch.

It is impossible to think along with the police investigators as to their motives and logic in having ignored Nelson's actual description of the killer. Decades later a retired officer familiar with the case said that investigators had located a witness to the Wiles murder in a softball player in a game near the railroad platform. However, without regard for what that witness might have told them in no way explains or justifies manipulating Norman Nelson's description of the killer. To send the police and members of the community on a wild goose chase for the wrong offender is senseless on every level.

Therefore it is more understandable that the police – apart from the investigators responsible for the sketch generation – would have been unlikely to associate the presence of a crime pattern early on in the continuing offenses. The forest preserve rape, while a serious offense, was a far lower profile offense than the Wiles murder. Therefore, for the general police population the first offense to come to their attention committed by the clean-cut, intelligent suspect would have been the forest preserve rape.

Of course, all of the subsequent non-fatal sexual attacks did contain common descriptions and a common method of operation. Recall, however, that police authorities specifically denied the existence of either a serial offender or a crime pattern. It is notable that the comment about the possibility of a serial offender came from patrol officers assigned to the Cappos murder and was not an official department statement from either the investigators or administration.

Cold Case Investigation

The information about the two murders and apparent serial rapes came to the attention of a cold case investigator who was working on another homicide in the same town. In the course of searching for a suspect in the other case all of the information contained herein was learned.

Catherine Cappos' brother had stayed in close contact with the police. To the best of his information investigators never advanced their investigation to the point where they actually conducted a suspect interrogation. At one point the brother asked whether the police had ever considered that both his sister and Margaret Wiles had been killed by the same individual. The police replied that there were absolutely no similarities between the two crimes.

One might argue that the following features were present in both murders:
1) Both were attacked with a knife.
2) The two crimes took place less than one mile from one another.
3) One victim was naked from the waist down, the other had her shorts pulled down.
4) Norman Nelson's description of the Wiles killer was remarkably similar to that of Catherine Cappos' killer.

5) Both murders clearly had a sexual nature.
6) The six years between the two murders were bridged by some 35 apparent serial rapes committed by an offender fitting the descriptions of the killer(s).

Crime Features

Serial offenders are essentially compulsive offenders in that they are driven to act. Individuals driven by sexual compulsions lack free choice as to when or where to commit a given act. A certain set of emotional conditions come together that require that the offender acts out in such a way so that he lacks free will to choose between committing the act or not.

It was this condition that would imply that the offender approached Margaret Wiles with the intention of sexually attacking her. Clearly, he had either ordered her to remove her clothing below the waist or he may have actually removed them himself. In either case he was interrupted in his plans on the arrival of Norman Nelson at the train station.

Since the sexual motive for the crime was not met and satisfied, it is most reasonable to believe that the same unsatisfied actor would seek another victim as soon as possible, in this case the next day in a nearby forest preserve.

Periodic Nature of Acts

The 35 or so rapes attributed to a serial offender took place over a six-year period. All took place between May and early October of the year, and all occurred out of doors. During one summer

116

there were no offenses matching the crime pattern in question.

A basic function of criminal investigation analysis is to create a framework that provides logical answers to known case facts. There are several possible explanations for the fact that the offenses occurred only during warm-weather months in the Midwestern climate:

1) The offender had occasion to be present in the area only during that time of year. Recall that he was frequently described as looking like a college student. Perhaps he was away at school during the remainder of those years.

2) The offender may have been "triggered" to sexually attack only when prospective victims wore lightweight outerwear. Perhaps females wearing bulky winter clothing failed to provide the offender with an impetus to attack.

3) Perhaps the offender was not comfortable acting out the sexual attack requirements while outside in the cold.

4) It is possible that whatever twisted incidents from his past, which caused him to sexually attack, took place in warm-weather settings. Thus his desire to act would occur in a similar setting.

5) The one year in which no offenses took place might be the result of the offender having been incarcerated for a similar or different act.

6) The answer to the timetable of offenses might have been circumstantial in nature; for example, he might have lived part time with

each of his parents. Perhaps there might be a similar crime pattern in another city halfway across the country.

<u>Failed Case Analysis</u>

*Recognition of the Crime Pattern*

The police might be forgiven if they failed to recognize the existence of a crime pattern as the description and behaviors of the offender were not clear-cut. In the event that they were not observing sex offenses where the victims survived their attacks, they may not have associated those offenses with the Wiles murder. This statement would be especially true to the extent that they were of the opinion that Wiles' killer was an older, sinister-looking fellow. However, the fact remains that there is an obvious link from the Wiles murder to the rape in the forest preserve, and so on.

*The Criminal Trail*

1) Margaret Wiles' sexually motivated attack/murder.
2) Forest preserve rape the very next day.
3) Multiple Jogging Track rapes.
4) Multiple street rapes with same offender description.
5) Catherine Cappos' murder near the last set of rapes.
6) Thus a strong possibility of connectedness in the murders exists.

*The Composite Sketch Farce*

The obvious reason for the creation of a composite sketch is to utilize a witness' information as a means of learning what a criminal offender

118

looks like. In this case the investigators did essentially the opposite. They went through the motions of having Norman Nelson describe the killer, but at the same time ignored what the witness was telling them. This begs the question of under just what conditions might the investigators have behaved in that way.

Since the investigators arrived at the hospital in the company of the sketch artist, there had to have been some sort of agreement in place that the artist was to ignore the description of the offender supplied by Nelson and instead draw a rendition of an older, more mature suspect who looked nothing whatsoever like the actual offender.

It is difficult to fathom a circumstance whereby police investigators would intentionally manipulate evidence away from the truth. Certainly, there could be no advantage to the investigators to lead information away from locating the actual killer. Yet, according to Norman Nelson, that is precisely what they did.

Whatever their motive, the manipulation of the composite sketch acted to effectively prevent easy subsequent recognition of the existence of a crime pattern and the apparent work of a serial offender.

*The Arson Lead Ignored*

Many murders are solved because somebody knows who did it and has a good reason for telling what they know. This is apparently just what was in the process of happening at the time that a former boyfriend attempted to set his former girlfriend's house on fire. She had long known that he had behaved suspiciously at the time that Margaret Wiles was killed but did not become ready to tell about it until he tried to set her house on fire.

However, when told about it, the lead investigator arrogantly ignored the lead on its face and did not do so much as speak to the information source or take other steps to link the suspect to the crime. Based on the nature of this event, it is impossible to attempt to make sense of the investigator's inaction other than to say that he practiced the worst possible type of failure to take proper police actions.

Formulating a Cold Case Plan

Now that it has been established as to just why the case was not initially solved by police investigators, the next step is to establish an effective means by which a 30-year-old case may be solved. The first step in this process must be to review what is known or believed to be true about the killer.

1) Serial offenders are compulsive criminals who tend to repeat their crimes until eventually caught by the police.

2) There was an abrupt halt to the sexual attack pattern immediately after the Catherine Cappos murder, indicating that the killer moved elsewhere, at least for a time.

3) Since such compulsions drive serial sex offenders to act, it is reasonable to consider that the killer was eventually arrested for an

120

offense at least somewhat similar to the rape pattern.

4) The offender's clean-cut appearance and apparent intelligence separate him from other criminal suspects commonly connected to a street crime culture.

5) Serial offenders typically spend a great deal of time in the commission of their attacks. Certain acts connected to the crime must be accomplished in order to enjoy their work. Note that in the Cappos attack, despite the public nature of the stabbing in an alley near witnesses, the killer still took the time to pull the victim's shorts down. Thus a sexual component to the offense was accomplished despite insufficient time to complete a rape attack.

6) The offender's willingness to always return to the same area, nearly 40 times over six years, demonstrates the defiance often seen in serial offenders, daring the police to catch him.

---

Search Tools

One recurring theme in this work is the fact that searching for suspects of unknown identity is greatly complicated by the passing of time. Had the police conducted a canvass of the community where the various crimes had taken place, it is likely that somebody would have come in contact with a clean-cut, intelligent, well-spoken young man fitting a certain physical description. He either resided

121

somewhere near the crimes or he traveled to and from his attacks. Somebody would have noticed him and probably would have been able to add some piece of information about him as well: where he stood waiting for public transportation, that he was seen entering a small red auto, or any variation thereof.

Someone would have recalled something about the suspect back at the time of the offenses. By contrast, cold case investigators would be unable to search for that variety of information in that absolutely nobody is about to recall having run into such a person thirty years earlier.

Perhaps a good starting point would be to confirm that all of this was indeed the work of a serial offender. That might be accomplished without much difficulty. Recall that there was a witness in each of the murders: Norman Nelson knows what the train station attacker looked like, and someone sitting on his front porch saw the individual who followed Catherine Cappos into the alley where she was killed. There are also countless other witnesses as well. Although with the passing of decades the multiple rapes could no longer be prosecuted, many of the witnesses might be located and asked to describe their respective attacker.

Thus the simple plan would be to have Norman Nelson describe the attacker to a graphic artist and then compare the results with the sketch of the killer of Catherine Cappos. Those sketches would then be shown to the various rape victims, who might confirm or refute that there was in fact a serial offender on the loose for over six years.

If that was confirmed, the cold case investigators could then focus their attention on the search for a full-blown serial offender who could be prosecuted for the two murders decades after the fact.

Serial offenders do not simply awake one day as a young adult and begin sexual and physically violent acts. Rather, such pathologies are progressive in nature, usually manifesting themselves during pre-teen years. Thus the sought-after offender would have come to the attention of neighbors, school and police officials for involvement with sex-oriented offenses.

In the event that the cold case investigation was being conducted by police personnel, they would have access to old juvenile records. Perhaps the serial offender grew up in the same town where the majority of offenses took place. Or they might check with authorities in nearby communities in search of decades of old juvenile sex offenses. Investigators would not have difficulty in tracing the suspect's acts into adulthood. Mugshots would be on file that might be viewed to determine whether or not any given individual might fit the physical description of the bright, clean-cut appearing offender.

Civilian investigators do not have access to police records and therefore must be extremely clever in gathering other data that is public access information. When searching for serial offenders, old newspaper articles often disclose important leads. However, media accounts of crimes do not include the names of juvenile offenders unless the suspect is charged criminally as an adult and sent to the criminal justice system. Thus a civilian search for events having occurred in the years before the Margaret Wiles murder would not disclose the identity of offenders under the age of seventeen.

In general terms newspaper searches for serial offenders may be undertaken in the following manner:

1) Since serial killers typically continue to act until arrested, it is reasonable to being the search at an age when the offender would have been a teenager.

2) Begin the search in the community where the offense occurred, as well as all adjoining towns or cities.

3) Collect articles about any crimes that are similar to the serial offenses in any way.

4) Categorize collected articles according to whether the offenses were solved or not.

5) Search for a pattern in the articles depicting offenses.

6) Compile a list of offenders arrested for similar acts.

7) Search for follow-up stories about the criminal trial for each similar offense.

8) Prison inmate information is public access information. Most states have websites containing particulars of the crimes

committed, along with a prison intake photo of the inmate.

9) There are times when cold case investigators may gather information indicating that a suspect arrested and charged for one offense may have also committed other offenses for which they were not charged at the time of the actual offenses.

10) It is thusly possible to identify a strong suspect in the above manner.

---

There needs to be a discussion as to the assertion that this particular serial offender did indeed continue committing offenses as certain earlier statements might seem to contradict that position. Recall that the six-year pattern of sex-related attacks upon women took place in a manner that might seem to argue against the contention that the offenses were continuous in nature. Consider,

1) All the offenses took place in warm-weather months.

2) During one entire summer there were no such offenses at all.

While the above facts clearly state that the offender did not act continuously over the given six-year period, there are unknown variables that might account for the lulls in the attacks. Most importantly, the offender may have been locked up over the one summer when there were no attacks in the community in question. Or he may have been carrying out similar attacks in another place. As to the seasonal nature of the attacks, there are three reasonable explanations for the lack of cold weather crimes. The first is that the offender may only be "triggered" to act during warm weather. Perhaps his sexual quirk is attached to a view of women dressed in summer attire. Second, it might be that he is simply uncomfortable attacking in chilling weather. The third possibility is that the offender winters elsewhere, possibly he was attending college in another city, or he split his time between living with various family members. Thus the investigation continues with the belief that it is correct and proper to seek a serial offender.

It is wise to search files not only in the city where most of the crimes occurred but in adjoining areas as well. Clearly, criminal offenders are seemingly not confined to the geographic boundaries of a jurisdiction. Recall that in this case not all of the "jogger rapes" occurred in the same city.

Although most serial offenses are identifiable by their method of operation, it is important to understand that the manner of the multiple offenses are more likely to be generally alike and not identical to one another. Since serial offenders are driven to act, they are not ordinarily able to plan their attacks in advance in the way that, say, an armed robber might. Thus the serial offender is usually called upon to improvise certain aspects of the crime. For example, his favorite location to attack might be a solitary outdoor area; however if a particular potential victim gains his arousal, he may have to carry out the crime in a train station or perhaps in a city alley. Despite the above-required differences in approach or actions, there are still likely to be certain common threads of behavior. Note that in another case treated in this work the offender felt it necessary to use a dull cutting object on the buttocks of his victims.

---

*In the course of a conversation about gathering newspaper files of crimes in order to construct a crime analysis pattern, it is significant to recognize that this is precisely the manner of gathering all of the information presented on the Wiles/Cappos murders and the serial rapes. Newspaper articles were used exclusively as a means of gaining information as to both the methods of operation and physical description of the offender.*

*Each of those crimes was then plotted both geographically and in a time line to chart their obvious similarities. Cleared by arrest offenses resulted in gathering photos and criminal history profiles of arrested offenders. Suspended (unsolved) cases were compared to cleared offenses as a means of determining what, if any, other offenses identified offenders may have committed.*

*The positive results disclosed that two murders and as many as 35 rape offenses are likely to have been the work of a single offender. The negative aspect of the work is that no strong suspects were identified as the result of this research. Not even one of the sex offenders charged with other offenses closely resembled the sought-after offender wanted in conjunction with the crime pattern. It is to be noted that the individual whose offenses most closely resembled the method of operation in the crime pattern was eliminated as the suspect in that he was in custody during many of the offenses.*

---

Information Gathering in
This Crime Pattern

The first round of searching of articles about sexual offenses was for the six-year period beginning with the Wiles murder, carrying on through the period of serial rapes, and ending with the Cappos murder. Over that period of time there were a dozen rape arrests and another forty sex offenses not attributed to the serial offender by the cold case investigators. Profiles on each of the arrested offenders were conducted and prison release photos were obtained of each. None of the offenders fit the physical description of the serial offender, and the methods of operation were extremely varied among the arrestees, none of which were similar to the work of the serial offender.

However, one suspect came to the attention of the cold case investigators as the result of their work on a different case in the same community within the same context. In that case a young woman was sexually attacked and murdered in her apartment. Clearly, this offense that occurred indoors was not similar to the crime pattern offenses; however, he came to the attention of the investigators as they continued to expand the years researched.

Once no suspects were forthcoming within the initial six-year search, the research was expanded to three years before the Wiles murder and three years after the Cappos murder, thus an overall twelve-year period was viewed. As additional sex offenders were researched and eliminated, the search was again increased until all known offenses over a twenty-year span were considered.

The suspect in question kidnapped a woman from an alley in the middle of the winter seven years after Catherine Cappos was killed in another nearby alley. In the kidnapping, the offender forced the victim into his own auto and drove her from one place to another, repeatedly raping her. He was arrested due to a good piece of police work and was sentenced to a ninety-year prison term.

Cold case investigators have yet to gain a photo of this suspect taken during the time period of the serial offenses, so it remains uncertain whether or not he fit the description of the serial offender. He is also a bit older than the serial offender was thought to have been at the time of the crime pattern. For both of those reasons this suspect does not qualify as an extremely strong suspect. However, that in no way means that he may not have been the serial offender. In any case, he needs to be either eliminated or condemned as the offender.

---

One of the primary premises of criminal investigation is, "when stuck, start over." The crime pattern is a prime example of that statement. Relative probability is such that it is highly unlikely that the serial offender was never arrested, either for a sex-related offense or another offense where his motive was tied to sex. It is possible that cold case researchers missed an article about such an arrest or perhaps the newspapers did not cover the arrest incident. It is also possible that he was arrested in another area of the country. If so, such records would be available to only law enforcement agencies and not to civilian cold case investigators.

Thus, this obvious crime pattern remains Unsolved/Suspended.

# CASE 5

## STREET ANSWERS

<u>Investigative Overview</u>

Inner-city crime is different from all other criminal incidents. In many such communities the surest statement possible is that "Crime is Normal." In certain years 95% of all killings in Michigan occur within Detroit. Certain city blocks in most major cities have literally scores of murders on an annual basis.

In such places the weather seldom has an opportunity to wash away blood from the streets before it is replaced by another deadly attack. One result of this constant bloodshed is that the public nature of street offenses attunes residents to great collective awareness of exactly who did what violent act. Particulars surrounding violence become common knowledge.

Thus the police must seek their answers where the killings occur – on the street.

# CASE 5

## The Crime

Jonathan Brodnax was a 13-year-old honor student who was to begin the eighth grade in the fall. He was riding his BMX bike on the busy urban street next to the housing project where he lived with his mother and four siblings.

Witnesses said that an older maroon Chevrolet sedan drove by and let go with a volley of bullets, which scattered a group of street gang members standing on the corner in front of a pool hall. Jonathan Brodnax took three rounds in the side, which seemingly had been intended for the gang members. The car used in the murder was abandoned several blocks away in between the gang boundaries of the apparent intended targets and that of the suspected shooters. The car had been stolen from another neighborhood the morning before the crime. No physical evidence was found within the car.

People on the street told slightly varying accounts of the shooting, however what was certain was that the victim had been riding his bike eastbound on Forty-third Street and the Chevrolet was west-bound when a passenger began firing out of the rear window on the driver's side. Both the driver and shooter wore hoodies that hid their profiles from the witnesses, therefore it was not too surprising that nobody recognized the offenders.

The Brodnax case was a true "heater case," in that everyone seemingly capable of taking a breath was demanding justice for Jonathan. The school board was busy counting public school children killed by gunfire, community members were irate that the case had not been solved in the "First 48" as per the television show theme, and the victim's pastor was on television every five minutes wondering out loud why the case was unsolved.

Early Investigation

The police took statements from over forty individuals who had been out on the street at the time of the shooting. This included more than a dozen admitted street gang members. Nobody had a clue about the possible motive for the apparent gang-related killing in which an innocent kid had been riddled with bullets in the street on his bike.

From the police point of view there was something very wrong with this turn of events. When the highly unusual occurs within the context of a crime, once the reason for the strange condition is understood the crime solution usually follows. Here, the problem was that street gang members are usually more than happy to become witnesses to the crimes of their rivals. They know who their rivals are and they typically know precisely why they were under attack. However, in this case none of that was true. Nobody knew anything.

Police spoke to the mother who showed them the child's honor roll awards and said how he never caused her any problems, except for his habit of staying outside their building long past curfew. Investigators confirmed that Jonathan had never come to the attention of the police. School officials told more of the same; when classmates were busy arguing about nonsense as kids will do, the victim would sit quietly reading a library book. He was more than willing to tell anyone who would listen that he planned on becoming the wealthiest person to ever come from his neighborhood.

Investigators showed photos of the suspected gang members in the area from which the maroon Chevrolet had been stolen but nobody had seen anything. Next, the gang members were picked up and questioned; all told the same story, they had no current problems with the gang from in front of the pool hall and therefore had no motive for the crime. Many of the suspects willingly offered alibis for the time of the shooting. Based on all of the above, the investigation was getting nowhere fast.

Positive Turning Point

The case was now two weeks old when the police stopped by to reassure Mrs. Brodnax that they were still working on the case. She offered the investigators a coke and accepted their compliment on the nice furnishings in her apartment. One of the investigators mentioned to her that she might pick up the bike that Jonathan had been riding at the time of his death. She declined, pointing to several more BMX bikes in the corner of the kitchen. "My other kids have their own bikes. It would hurt too much to see that bike again. Why don't you give it to a child who could use it?" The investigator explained that she would have to stop by the police station to sign Jonathan's bike out of inventory.

The investigators went back to the station and looked up the inventory slip for the bike. They got its serial and model numbers and traced the bike to the shop where it had been purchased. The lady behind the counter was shown a crime scene photo in which the bike was resting alongside the young victim. She immediately recognized the victim whom she referred to as "Little Jon Jon." "That little boy was one of my very best customers. I was worried that something like this would eventually happen to him," she said.

The shop owner went on to explain that Jonathan Brodnax had bought his first BMX from her perhaps three years earlier, which would have made him ten years old at that time. He paid $800 cash for a midnight black model. He had told her that his father was a famous criminal attorney and often gave him money to buy the things he wanted. At first the bike lady believed that story, but as he returned ten or twelve more times, she became certain that he was involved in some sort of lucrative and probably dangerous business. Now the police investigators had a much better idea of why their little victim was out late beyond curfew.

To the Streets

The next day the investigators drove their unmarked squad car onto the black-top play lot alongside the project building where the victim had lived his entire life. The presence of the squad car immediately drew a half-dozen third-graders away from where they were throwing stones at an abandoned auto without wheels. "You the police or the FBI?" one of them wanted to know. The investigator didn't answer the question, instead asking one of his own: "Who did Jonathan Brodnax upset?"

The kids all began talking at once, but each in his own way, they were all asking how the investigator knew that someone was angry with the little victim. The investigator looked toward the kid who had asked if they were the FBI. "Jon Jon bought nice things for his mother and lots of bikes for his sisters, right?" Once again they all chattered at once, but what was confirmed was that Jonathan had worked for adult crack dealers delivering kilos on his BMX bikes. He did not deal with street gang members or their drug sales. Based on the kids' sketchy information it appeared as if Jonathan would meet a wholesaler at a given location, grab his bag, and immediately drop it off to one of several retailers.

None of the kids knew any specific information about who he was involved with other than the fact that one of their sisters claimed to have seen Jon Jon talking to an older white man near the big liquor store on Forty-third Street.

So much for the "innocent victim gunned down by gang crossfire" theory.

---

The investigators contacted narcotics officers to learn more about the inner workings of local street drug sales. White organized crime was said to supply kilo-quantities of powdered cocaine that were sold to wholesalers who then converted the coke into crack rocks. Bags and bags and bags of crack rocks were then sold on the streets in user quantities by a variety of retailers. The narcotics officers of course could not say just who the players were at the high end of the chain, otherwise they would have been charged by now. They were able to supply the homicide investigators with a few names of wholesalers from whom they had seized large quantities in recent search warrant raids. What it boiled down to was that the victim might have been working for any one of a couple dozen wholesalers.

It was also difficult to determine just how Jonathan Brodnax had wronged a dealer to the extent that he would have gunned down a 13-year-old in front of dozens of witnesses. Traditionally, when members of a criminal organization are killed by their own, it is nearly always due to the victim having either brought unwanted attention to the organization, or more often, because the victim ripped someone off.

In this case it was likely that the victim had stolen from a dealer, but the question was – on which end of the criminal chain. In the event that Jonathan's role was to deliver kilos on his bike to local wholesalers, the question would have been which dealer would have suffered the loss. If the wholesaler paid organized crime for the kilos in advance, then it would have been the wholesaler who suffered the loss. If the delivery were made prior to payment, then Jonathan's theft would have cost the organized crime supplier.

All of this made sifting through potential suspects extremely difficult in the sense that homicide investigators would be searching between Black inner-city dealers and white organized crime members. The two groups were sociologically a million miles away from one another.

Investigators began doing background checks on each of fourteen local dealers who had been the subject of a drug confiscation stemming from a search warrant raid over the past year. The first six subjects were unremarkable in the sense that nothing in their criminal past might have obviously linked them to Jonathan Brodnax. However, the seventh subject was of possible interest.

Monroe Winters was only nineteen and had been present when an adult woman named Lucille Dease had her home raided three months earlier. Police seized two kilos of uncut cocaine with a street value of $60,000. Dease was charged with possession with intent to distribute while Monroe Winters was charged with the misdemeanor offense of inmate of a disorderly house. At the first court appearance the pair was represented by Q. Andrew Filipek, one of the highest priced attorneys in town. A search of his juvenile records disclosed that Monroe Winters had grown up in the project building next door to where Jonathan Brodnax lived.

As a 16-year-old Monroe had been charged with possession and delivery of crack cocaine. The location of the arrest had been three blocks away from the pool hall where the murder had taken place. Though criminal patterns of advancement are not all the same, sixteen was younger than usual to be dealing on the street, and certainly not very many individuals still in their teens are often associated with kilo-quantity drug confiscations. Seemingly Monroe Winters was good at his trade.

The investigators fully understood that they had nothing in the way of tangible evidence against Winters, so picking him up for questioning would have been senseless. Instead, the investigators decided to vary from the usual method of information gathering, having made the decision to spend some time watching their new suspect. They went to the department motor pool and picked out a work-van that would not attract undue attention. They parked up the street from Lucille Dease's house and didn't have to wait very long. An old Buick tricked out with spinner rims pulled up in front of the house, and a tall, thin kid who looked far younger than his years walked down the porch steps and into the car. The driver wore a white hoodie with black print so it was hard to see just what he looked like. The ride took less than ten minutes, and when the car parked they were less than two blocks away from where the stolen maroon Chevrolet had been.

One of the strongest axioms of criminal investigation is to always assume against the existence of coincidences until they are proven to be so. The case was either coming together or there were the following coincidences:

1) Monroe Winters dealt in kilos.
2) He grew up next door to the victim, thus would likely have known him.
3) The car used in the crime was taken from a location where the suspects had driven to.

---

Investigators ran the Buick's license plate that was registered to an Alfonso Bennett who lived at the address where the car was now parked. Bennett's criminal history sheet began with a string of auto thefts, before he graduated to a pair of aggravated batteries, and finally to an attempted murder for which he served four years. The police computer also disclosed another useful bit of information. The Buick had accumulated a dozen parking tickets, which meant that the car was to be booted and towed until the fines were paid. Once the pair walked inside a pink frame house, the investigators called for a patrol car to order the boot and tow it to the auto pond.

Five minutes later a patrol car with two female officers pulled to the curb right alongside the tow truck. Within seconds the car had been booted and the pair ran from the house screaming about the turn of events. Alfonso Bennett was yelling that he needed access to the car, that he needed to get his personal belongings. He was frantic. Monroe Winters told him to calm down, then Bennett whispered something to Winters. Soon he too was screaming. At that point the investigators got out of their van and went to the patrol officers' aid. By then the pair of suspects began threatening the police with bodily harm. Seconds later they were in handcuffs in the back seat of the squad car.

The Buick received special treatment. Instead of being towed to where ordinary cars are taken, this car went to a special garage with a variety of sensors and detectors. The investigators then spent an hour putting together a search warrant to go through the Buick, which was quickly approved. Drug and gun-sniffing dogs were summoned to the garage. Police quickly recovered a Colt .9mm pistol with a half-empty clip, and not long after, a hidden trap door that contained three kilos of 96% pure powdered cocaine. The best part was that the investigators did not need to go searching for their suspects; they were already at the station charged with having threatened the patrol officers.

Who Gets Charged With What?

The weapon recovered from inside the Buick might have been the murder weapon, but it would be a day or so before that could be established. The wounds to Jonathan Brodnax had been through and through, meaning that they entered and then exited his body, thus were not to be found within him. However, the crime lab did recover three slugs from the base of the front of the pool hall building. To the naked eye they might have come from either a .38 or .9mm. One shell casing was recovered from the middle of the street where the drive-by car had traveled.

In the meantime police investigators had a chance to wrap the case up through skillful interrogation. Intelligent police questioning is based on the investigator's ability to confront the suspect with the known facts of the crime that incriminate the suspect. In this case the police knew that Monroe Winters had grown up living next door to the victim and had clearly graduated to a big-time dealer. They also knew that the victim had been riding expensive bikes for the past three years, and was given to staying out late at night when much drug dealing occurs. Taken as one, it would appear that the youthful victim had been working for Winters for years.

Less was known about Alfonso Bennett's role, however the investigators were not without information. Bennett owned a Buick with a hidden compartment that contained enough drugs to assure him of many years in prison. He also was linked to the murder by virtue of the fact that the stolen car used in the murder had been taken from near Bennett's house. Throw in the possession of the gun inside the car, and he was in a whole lot of trouble.

Felons in trouble need all the help they can get, and the greatest gift to Bennett would be for him to avoid also being charged with Jonathan Brodnax's murder. A commonly held interrogation formula is to seek information from less-involved parties in order to gain evidence against the most-involved offender. For example, the getaway driver who waited in the car gets a chance to turn evidence on the robber who killed the sales clerk in the crime. However, this case was a bit more complicated in the sense that the police actually had no idea whether Bennett was directly involved in the murder or not.

---

## The Bennett Interrogation

The pair of investigators drank coffee while Alfonso Bennett had a soft drink. They took his handcuffs off his thin wrists, then handed him the Revised Statutes Book opened to the page containing the charge, "Possession of a Controlled Substance with Intent to Deliver."

*Interrogator:* Read the last line under the heading "Penalty."

*Suspect:* Not less than ten years nor more than thirty.

*Interrogator:* That's a long time to go away for holding Monroe's dope bag.

*Suspect:* You going to tell him you think it's my bag?

*Interrogator:* We know it's his bag. He's a dealer, not you.

*Suspect:* How do you figure that?

*Interrogator:* Monroe started out as a PeeWee, acting as lookout for dealers. He was smart so he moved up fast. He knew Jon Jon from the projects and bought him his first BMX bike so that he could be the new lookout. When

Monroe graduated to becoming a retailer, he brought Jon Jon along with him. Monroe would pay up front for his kilos, then have Jon Jon pick the packages up on his bike and deliver them to Lucille's house where he kept his stuff. Only the last time around Jon Jon kept the kilos for himself and probably sold them to the competition. So after warning the kid to come up with the kilos, Monroe and someone else did a drive-by with the Chevy you stole and blew the kid away.

*Suspect:* You got the whole thing figured out except I had nothing to do with any of that.

*Interrogator:* You can say that every day for the next twenty years doing your Intent to Deliver.

*Suspect:* You know those kilos are too rich for my blood.

*Interrogator:* Your Buick, your hidden compartment, and your dope bag. That's how it goes down.

*Suspect:* I agree. That's how it does go down. Except I didn't kill that kid.

*Interrogator* Convince us.

*Suspect:* In return for what?

*Interrogator:* We could talk to the prosecutor and ask her to package the gun and dope into concurrent time. Plead guilty,

|              | take the twenty, and you could be out in less than ten years. Just fill in the blanks on the drive-by. |
| *Suspect:*   | Call in the prosecutor and have her tell me she'll do what you just said she might. |

The Felony Charging Process

In many large jurisdictions there are special units within the prosecutor's office whose job it is to respond to police facilities to access the strength of evidence against criminal suspects. When police investigators seek felony charges, they contact the Felony Review Unit who go to the police station and interview the police, witnesses, and suspects to the extent that they are willing to waive their Miranda rights and discuss the case.

In this case the police investigators laid the groundwork for a plea-bargaining arrangement between Alfonso Bennett and the State, whereby the suspect would turn State's evidence in a murder case in return for certain considerations on the part of the prosecutor's office.

Once the Felony Review prosecutor arrived, Bennett repeated his conversation held earlier with the police investigators. He then introduced a new piece of information. "You figured out just about everything, but I know one thing that you don't know. Tell me you'll work with me and I'll ice your case," Bennett said.

The prosecutor told him that they would not charge him with the Unlawful Use of Weapons case, and that they would allow him to plead guilty to possession of the drugs found in the car, rather than possession with intent to deliver. Everybody then shook hands.

Bennett explained that the driver in the killing was Lucille Dease's brother named Owen Wells, and Monroe Winters had been the trigger-man. But what Bennett told them next was even more interesting: As they were making good their getaway, they were stopped in traffic by a double-parked car. Winters jumped out of the car and screamed at the driver of the car blocking their way. Owen Wells then jumped out of the getaway car to see what was going on. It turned out that the little old lady double-parked was a lady named Miss Miller, who had taught Winters in the third grade. The pair apologized to her and then was able to drive around her and on their way to ditch the stolen car.

---

The police investigators quickly found Miss Miller who stated that she had known Monroe Winters since he started elementary school, and that he sure did jump out of a maroon Chevrolet at a time that was five minutes after shots fired from that car killed Jonathan Brodnax. She soon after identified Owen Wells as having been the driver of the same car. That testimony, along with Alfonso Bennett's testimony that Monroe Winters had told him all about the killing, convicted both killers, despite the fact that they both invoked Miranda and refused to talk to the police.

# CASE 6

# INVESTIGATIVE TUNNELVISION

<u>Investigative Overview</u>

At the outset of a criminal investigation it is common practice to analyze the known case facts as a means of creating a theory to explain what is known. Such speculation should occur at the outset of the investigation and be tested through intelligent inquiry. As such, speculative theories are typically proven or invalidated within hours or days.

In this case a young woman encountered a man in a supermarket and was found raped and murdered a few hours later. In between those events an off-duty police officer saw her being driven in her own car by a male.

The police investigator then concocted the theory that the victim was killed by someone she knew well, as she would have not allowed a stranger to drive her fancy sports car. That theory was maintained for over a decade of failed investigation, in that only investigative leads were considered which held that the crime had been a relationship-based murder.

# CASE 6

<u>The Crime – Jennifer Rowe</u>

The victim was an extremely attractive young woman who worked as an attorney for a government organization. She had been raised in Kansas and moved east after law school graduation. She was found naked in an elementary school playground. The victim had been shot in the back of the head from close range. Autopsy findings would later disclose the presence of semen within the vaginal track. It was determined that the sexual attack had taken place subsequent to the shooting, thus her killer effectively engaged in sexual intercourse with much of the victim's head missing. Her jeans, blouse, and underwear were neatly folded alongside her remains. Her red flat shoes were arranged next to her clothing.

The school was located in a residential area. Several residents would state that they had heard what sounded like a single gunshot, however nobody had bothered to call the police.

<u>Early Investigation</u>

The victim's shiny sports car was found in a supermarket parking lot the following morning. The interior of the car was immaculate except for a single bag of groceries in the rear seat and a box cutter on the rear floor. The register receipt indicated that the victim had paid for the groceries at 9:10 p.m. There were no security tapes available that might provide investigators with information as to the comings and goings of the victim's car.

151

Police responded to the presence of the box cutter with the logical theory that perhaps a supermarket employee might have been inside the victim's car in that such tools are commonly used by grocery stock clerks. Investigators interviewed nearly two hundred male employees before deciding that six workers qualified as potential suspects. Each voluntarily gave blood samples for DNA comparisons. All were eliminated as the donors of the semen within Jennifer Rowe.

A second lead surfaced less than one day after the crime. Some twenty minutes after the victim had passed through the supermarket checkout line, an off-duty police officer saw the victim in her car. The car was moving slowly and erratically, jumping a curb while making a right-hand turn from one side-street onto another. Perhaps ninety feet down the street the car came to a stop and the victim got out of the passenger-side door. She then stood alongside the car speaking to whoever was behind the wheel through the open window.

The off-duty officer assumed that the victim was being dropped off there and drove away toward the police station. He was in uniform at the time of the incident, and his car arrived at the stop sign across from the victim's car. Thus whoever was inside the victim's car may have been able to make out the fact that he was a uniformed officer.

Investigative Error 1

The police investigators took the off-duty officer's account of events and arrived at the theory that the victim had been killed by a former lover

152

because she would not have allowed a stranger to drive her new sports car.

That the victim had been dropped off where the officer saw her standing by the car was pure speculation. In order to determine if that theory was correct, all the police needed to do was canvass the block where the victim had been seen. If anyone on the block knew the victim, then she was doubtless dropped off there. If nobody on the block knew her, then the police assumption was worthless. Unfortunately, the police investigators never did interview the area residents. However, had anyone been paid a visit just before her death, he/she would have been certain to have initiated contact with the police.

Another question tied to the theory that she was killed by a lover/former lover also calls for an answer: If the killer did drop the victim off on that street, should one then also assume that he later returned there to pick her up later? And that he later drove to the school yard where he then killed and raped her? Most unlikely.

A point is therefore arrived at where:

1) If the off-duty officer was wrong in his belief that the victim was actually being dropped off, then

2) Investigators would have no logical basis for their belief that the victim was killed by someone close to her.

3) All subsequent assumptions based on initially faulty conclusion must also be faulty as well.

No wonder that the case remained unsolved in the months that followed.

---

Six months later two college students, Chris Melton and Tim Quack, went to a bar in a nearby urban setting to celebrate the end of finals week. As they walked to her car, they were approached by an armed gunman who forced the pair into her car and instructed them to drive to an isolated wooded area that was thirteen miles from the schoolyard where Jennifer Rowe had been executed then raped.

Once out of the victim's car, the gunman shot Tim Quack point-blank in the back of the head. Chris Melton immediately tried running away into the brush, but she was quickly caught and likewise shot in the back of the head, then undressed and raped. Her clothing was found neatly folded next to her red shoes.

Investigative Error 2

Police investigators from adjoining counties met and must have looked at the following facts:

1) Both female victims were shot in the head, then raped.
2) Both female victims wore red shoes.
3) The respective crimes took place thirteen miles apart from one another, a five-minute drive.
4) The crimes occurred six months apart.

In one of the most difficult to understand investigative findings ever, the respective police agreed that the crimes were clearly not connected. They based their decision on the fact that Jennifer Rowe was Black and Chris Melton, White. Additionally, the first victim had been alone, while the second was with Tim Quack.

---

### Investigative Error 3

A month after the Melton-Quack killings, Chris Melton's mother received a New York City parking ticket issued the day after the crime, on the street of a major city, in front of a public housing project. Investigation disclosed that the car had been looted and set ablaze while still in front of the building. No evidence was found within the car. The distance between where the crime occurred and where the car was ticketed was 300 miles.

Despite the fact that the killer had clearly used the car to get to the projects, the investigating police never traveled to that city in an attempt to learn what known offenders in or around that housing project might have been in the area of the murders.

### Investigative Error 4
*Questioning Police Logic*

During the latter stages of the first year after Jennifer Rowe was killed investigators continued to search for ex-boyfriends past and present. The problem was, of course, that normal people when broken up will seldom act as did her killer, and the killer of Chris Melton and Tim Quack as well. In stalker-related murders, which is what the police

155

insisted had occurred, offenders seek out their victims, usually in a public place, and move quickly most often armed with a firearm, killing the victim without regard for witnesses. For these reasons stalker murders are most often easily solved.

By contrast, the crimes in question had features, which were literally the opposite of the common behaviors of a jilted lover who kills:

1) The crimes clearly began with abductions, a time-consuming act.
2) The victims were executed by gunshots to the head.
3) The dead female victims were then disrobed, which would have taken much time.
4) The offender then had sex with the dead body missing much of its skull.
5) Their clothing was neatly folded beside their remains.
6) Their red shoes were found sitting alongside their folded clothing.

Two points became quite apparent: The killer conducted the crimes in perhaps the most time-consuming manner possible, and the depth of his twisted desires was all-consuming. All of the behaviors connected to these crimes scream "serial killer."

Crimes without apparent motives are often the work of an offender who stands alone in knowing its hidden motive. In order for serial offenders to enjoy their work, there are certain aspects of method of operation that must be accomplished. In these companion cases the folding of the female victims' clothing was purposeful and highly symbolic to the offender.

Of greater significance is the fact that the female victims were sexually assaulted after having been shot point-blank in the head. Such behavior is so far from the norm that to attach such behavior to an individual other than a "criminal freak" is pure folly. Individuals driven to such acts are going to continue committing such offenses until caught.

The "trigger" in both cases was clearly the fact that the victims each wore red shoes. Something in the killer's past was linked to an encounter or encounters with a woman wearing red shoes. As such the red shoes act as the motive for the offenses within the mindset of the killer.

When "triggered" or driven to act, serial offenders have no choice but to respond to whatever twisted thought drives them to act. This means that the serial offender may have to be adaptive to conditions surrounding the intended victim. The police were dead wrong when they thought that the race of the two female victims would have mattered to a serial offender; it didn't. All that mattered was that both wore red shoes. Similarly, the fact that Chris Melton was with Tim Quack at the time that the killer saw her was a mere complication. Having killed Jennifer Rowe six months earlier, along with the knowledge that he was about to kill Chris under any circumstances, his having to kill the young man first was a simple adaptation that was nothing more than a minor complication.

*A New Lead Surfaces*

Just a year after the Jennifer Rowe crime the police were contacted by a married couple who related the following information:

1) They had been shopping in the supermarket on the evening of the crime.

2) The husband was in line at the deli counter with Jennifer Rowe.

3) She was approached by a clean-cut Black fellow who was clearly a stranger to her.

4) She smiled at his flirting but seemed to remain proper and reserved toward him.

5) The witness was waited on first and therefore left the victim and stranger at the counter.

6) Perhaps twenty minutes later the wife was standing in front of the market.

7) She saw the victim standing alongside her sports car talking to someone who obviously was the same individual her husband had seen talking to the victim earlier.

8) The victim did smile at the handsome stranger but also seemed to be looking around, perhaps in an effort to gain someone's attention.

9) The witnesses then loaded their groceries into their car and left.

---

Relevance of New Information

The investigative term "relative probability" deals with the proposition that given two choices of what may have occurred within the framework of the crime, one choice is often clearly the more reasonable perspective of events.

In this case relative probability states that it is more likely that Jennifer Rowe was killed by the stranger she encountered at the supermarket as opposed to the notion that she

1) Met the stranger at the supermarket,
2) Spoke to him both inside and outside the store,
3) Disengaged with him,
4) Then met someone else who later killed her.

It was important to attempt to learn just how well the victim and suspect were getting along, in that if she had clearly liked him, she might have voluntarily left the supermarket parking lot to go somewhere with him. By contract, if Jennifer were not about to be picked up by a stranger, then it would be safe to assume that she did not leave the parking lot with him voluntarily.

In order to make that determination, the investigators might have interviewed the cashier who waited on the victim. If the stranger was with her in the checkout line, perhaps she might have left with him. However, if she were alone in line, then it would have been safe to assume that she had told him that she was not interested in him, either verbally or by body language.

If she had disengaged from the suspect while inside the supermarket, then he would have had to approach the victim for the second time in the parking lot. Logically, if the victim had "blown him off" once, it is reasonable to assume that it was her intent to do the same thing again in the parking lot. Recall that the witness stated that the victim seemed to be looking around for help while speaking to the stranger. If so, it is also reasonable to believe that she sensed danger at that point.

Unfortunately the police investigators did not see fit to interview the supermarket cashier to determine whether or not the victim had passed through the checkout line alone.

Investigative Error 5

*Falling in Love with a Theory*

Recall that the investigators in the Jennifer Rowe case were convinced that she had been killed by someone she knew well because she would not have allowed a stranger to drive her car. This theory, of course, flies in the face of issues connected with kidnapping and carjacking. At the moment that she told the handsome stranger that she was leaving the parking lot, all he had to do was pull out his gun and force her into her own car.

However, one might have thought that the investigators would rethink their illogical theory once the new information about the handsome stranger in the supermarket came to their attention. Certainly the witness' account of the conversation at the deli counter made it perfectly clear that he was a total stranger to the victim. Thus, in order to do their work properly, they were required to search for the stranger; however, there is actually no indication that the investigators did follow that lead.

Instead, they traveled to Jennifer's hometown seeking a jilted lover who was also sick enough to have committed such a gruesome crime. Obviously, no such individual was to be found. That was not surprising in the sense that offenders given to acts such as having sex with a corpse missing much of its head do not normally also have a dating life. Flying in the face of all logic the investigators continued to search for a date-rape killer.

Over the following decade no new leads were forthcoming, if for no other reason than that they had failed to search for the handsome stranger.

Two Plus Two Equals . . .

Nearly twelve years after the crimes a lab technician decided to compare the semen within the two female victims, despite the fact that the respective investigators had long before announced that the crimes were not connected. The semen in the two victims matched. Whoever killed Jennifer Rowe and Chris Melton was indeed a serial killer.

What took place next is one of the most impossible investigative steps to explain. Within weeks of the announcement that the same offender had killed all involved, the Rowe investigators returned to interview more former boyfriends of the victim in her hometown. Thus the investigative logic had become:

1)   Jennifer Rowe was killed by a former boyfriend who investigators had not been able to locate over the past dozen years.

2)   The same individual who had killed Jennifer in a date-rape situation then kidnapped Chris

161

Melton and Tim Quack and killed the two strangers, thus completely having changed both his method of operation and motive for the second crime.

3) Though it was by then known that the killer in the second crime had forced the couple into their own car at gunpoint, the investigators disregarded the probability that he had taken control of Jennifer Rowe in precisely the same manner.

4) Rather, they continued to travel around the nation seeking a killer who the victim would have been glad to allow to drive her car.

A Decade of Futility

The investigative decision that the Rowe and Melton/Quack investigators had made that their crimes were unrelated made their respective tasks far more difficult, but not necessarily impossible. When two or more crimes are committed by the same individual or group of offenders, the risk is that the answer to one question is already a fact known by those working the other offense. However that does not absolutely preclude that fact being learned in another way by the investigative team.

For example, suppose that there are two separate home invasion robberies being investigated by separate investigators. Team A may learn that a silver blue truck was seen parked nearby the crime scene with its motor running. Team B may not know about that truck having been at the other crime, but they might have spoken to a suspect earlier in their own investigation who had driven a silver blue truck to the police station to speak to them. Had the two agencies shared information, both investigative teams would have known that the owner of the silver blue truck was actually a prime suspect in both crimes.

However, it would have been possible for the team who learned about the truck to have located its owner, such as seeking the truck as it was driven on the public way. Thus, working two or more crimes committed by common offenders becomes far easier when investigators understand that they are seeking serial offenders.

In this case the two investigative teams got absolutely nowhere, either individually or collectively, over the next decade.

A New Set of Eyes

A civilian cold case investigator was contacted by an interested party. His work soon caught the attention of local and national media. The cold case findings follow:

1) It was extremely likely that the "handsome stranger" was the killer in the Rowe case.
2) Former lovers/stalkers seldom sexually attack their victims.
3) The folding of Jennifer Rowe's clothes alongside her body was symbolic to her killer.
4) The treatment of the victim's clothing was a "screaming" method of operation.
5) The fact that the victim was first executed and then raped was such a twisted sequence of behaviors that such an individual would not

have been capable of a dating relationship with anyone.

6) The clearly great amount of time taken to commit the crime smacked of a serial killer.

7) What the police had failed to consider was that the killer had forced Jennifer into her own car at gunpoint.

8) The manner in which the killer was driving her car when seen by the off-duty officer was in keeping with the driver holding a gun on the victim while driving.

9) The victim was then ordered from the car still at gunpoint when seen by the off-duty officer.

10) The police failed to ask residents on the block, where the officer thought the victim was being dropped off, whether or not they knew Jennifer Rowe. If nobody knew her there, she had no reason for being dropped off, thus she was not dropped off there.

11) The notion that Jennifer Rowe was a "date-rape" victim was folly for two superb reasons: Women like the victim do not get naked and make love in school yards any more than they use a sound-truck to announce their actions; and as stated elsewhere, freaks who commit the type of crime in question do not date.

12) Once the second crime took place any knowledgeable investigator would have quickly noted that they had two dead women, both shot in the back of the head, then raped, both of whom wore red shoes, and both had their clothes nearly folded alongside their

respective bodies. SO THERE IS A SERIAL KILLER ON THE LOOSE.

13) Chris Melton's car was ticketed in an urban setting in a nearby state. In all probability the killer had driven the car to the public housing building where it was ticketed and walked inside the building to where someone close to him lived.

14) Thus the entire police investigation should have immediately been moved to that state until all actions toward locating the killer there had been exhausted.

15) The serial killer was likely to have continued to act until caught and either had been to prison and since released, or was still in prison for a nearly identical execution-rape on another female wearing red shoes.

---

The cold case findings were then presented to the investigators concerned with both separate investigations. The media asked them whether or not the two agencies had actually discussed the fact that both female victims had been wearing red shoes at the time of their respective deaths. The police investigators refused to answer the question.

Media members then asked the respective investigators whether they had contacted the FBI to include their cases in the federal crime profiling system, VICAP. Investigators said that they had no idea if that had been done but did concede that it seemed like an excellent idea.

## A Long Overdue Conclusion

Immediately upon having been confronted by the media as to their collective investigative inaction, both departments did contact the FBI and placed their cases in the VICAP system. Within only a matter of weeks VICAP had matched the Rowe and Melton/Quack killings to another crime two thousand miles away, for which the killer was awaiting execution on death row.

Tragically, a 15-year-old girl was walking home after dark from cheerleading practice when she was abducted at gunpoint and forced into a car. She was then driven at gunpoint to an isolated area where she was

1) Shot execution-style in the back of her head.
2) Raped after her death.
3) Her clothing was neatly folded alongside her body.
4) Her RED SHOES were next to her clothing.

---

## Case Prologue

Serial killers are created by failed police investigations. Had the police understood what the Jennifer Rowe crime was actually about, Chris Melton and her boyfriend, Tim Quack, could not have been killed. Likewise, had the two police agencies been bright enough to see that their respective crimes were the work of a serial offender, the little cheerleader all the way across the country could not have been killed either.

# CASE 7

## SUSPECT DOES NOT MATCH
## THE METHOD OF OPERATION

Investigative Overview

Stalker murders committed by scorn lovers all tend to be quite similar to one another in the sense that they nearly always occur quickly, are often public in nature, and seldom if ever have a sexual component. In stark contrast to the above description, serial killers take great time inflicting overkill wounds and much of the time do attack their victims sexually.

When Jayme Jackson was murdered nearby an outdoor skating rink, the police quickly learned that a former lover had made certain threats upon the victim when she broke up with him. The investigators did as they should have by attempting to link the ex-lover to the crime. However, nothing they did gave even the slightest indication that the suspect was guilty of the crime.

Despite the fact that Jayme Jackson had been mutilated by over sixty puncture wounds, the investigators did not consider that she may have been the victim of a serial offender.

# CASE 7

## The Crime

Jayme Jackson was found in the warm-up house of an ice skating rink in a well-known winter ski resort area. She had been strangled with a long scarf she wore around her neck. Her ski pants were in place, however her panties were found nearby on the ground. Her white insulated vest was open, and one of the snaps was sticking at an odd angle from the material. There were no signs of forcible rape, and later the autopsy would confirm that there had been no sexual attack.

There were more than sixty puncture wounds to the front of her torso, and her long blonde hair was tied together in a tight knot in a haphazard manner.

## Recognizing the Unusual

One of the keys to success in any criminal investigation is an ability to recognize and understand what is unusual, different, or out of place about a crime. In this instance the question is how did her underwear and outer clothing become separated? Perhaps she was forced at one point to disrobe.

If that is so, the second question then becomes under just what circumstances did her ski pants return to her body. Was she allowed by her attacker to put the pants back on, or did the killer dress her by himself after the crime? Four strands of the victim's hair were found on the warm-up house cement floor, all within inches of where her head rested. The victim's green wool sweater was blood-soaked in the front, but not to a great extent considering that the more than thirty puncture marks to her chest and stomach were each about four inches deep. The order of events of the attack was not totally explained by the autopsy as the listed cause of death was manual strangulation and stab wounds to the chest and stomach. There was no blood splattering as the victim's sweater caught the blood.

In this instance there was no mention in the police reports that investigators saw anything out of the ordinary, or at least they did not include any such thoughts in their reports.

---

Small-Town Homicide

Police investigators hone their craft through what they are taught by their partners and by the repetitive nature of working many cases. In major cities there may be anywhere from one homicide a week to as many as several a day. No wonder then that investigators in heavily populated urban areas usually become extremely effective before very long.

By contrast, suburban and rural violent crimes investigators may actually only have an opportunity to investigate a homicide once a year or in many instances far fewer than that. Fewer opportunities to learn often equal both a lack of experience and knowledge.

This condition then becomes complicated by another set of circumstances that also often hinders small-town investigators as well. Consider that:

1) Most murder victims are killed by someone they knew in life.
2) Such murders thus become solved by conducting a background investigation of the victim.
3) Many times someone in the victim's life surfaces as an individual with a motive for possibly having committed the crime.
4) By working that angle investigators are able to properly identify that suspect as the killer.

Also consider that relationship murders are not only most common but are also the easiest homicide offenses to solve. Thus it is not surprising that when the inexperienced investigator has solved a murder in the past, it was probably a relationship-based crime. Therefore, on the occasion of a subsequent murder perhaps months or years later, the inexperienced investigator will once again search along the same path. If a former lover or a neighbor killed the last victim, the inexperienced investigator will be searching in the same locations next time around, even if the killer's message says something totally different.

---

Early Investigative Turning Point

Police investigators looked into the victim's past and found that she had broken up with an individual who had continued to pursue her for

171

many months after. Several of the victim's close friends said that the former boyfriend did not scare her, that he simply continued to send her flowers and find many other ways to demonstrate his love for her.

He had no clear-cut alibi for the time of the crime, claiming to have been home alone a hundred miles away at her apparent time of death. Investigators spent weeks attempting to find a service station clerk or anyone else who might be able to place the ex-boyfriend in the town where the murder took place. No such witnesses were to be found.

The police called their suspect in for questioning on several occasions. The last time they interrogated him, investigators accused him of the crime; however, the police accusations were hollow in the sense that they had absolutely no evidence to back up the accusations. The ex-boyfriend then responded by retaining legal counsel, thus cutting off future interrogations.

Months went by during which time the police obtained their suspect's telephone records seeking information indicating that he might have hired the crime to be carried out. No such evidence was found. Investigators then kept their suspect under surveillance, however he did nothing to indicate that he had been involved in Jayme Jackson's death. And nothing came together.

---

A New Start

The first rule of cold case investigation is to begin as if the crime had taken place an hour before. Do not assume that anything that was said to have been investigated was done so in the proper manner. Do not accept as accurate other investigators' definitions of what a crime was about.

Thus it was that the victim's family asked a civilian investigator to look at the case.

The first step of the new investigation was to backtrack and look at the hours leading up to the victim's death. Police had found a business card in her pocket for an expensive hair salon less than a mile away from the skating rink where she was killed.

The stylist who had cut Jayme's hair had moved away months before so that she would have to be tracked down in order to learn what if anything the victim had talked about while her hair was being styled. However, the visit proved to have been far from a waste of time. The salon owner clearly recalled the victim having been there. The new investigator asked whether she might have recalled anything unusual or significant about the day of the crime. She responded by stating that the murder took place during a stretch of time in which a "very strange homeless type" had been hanging around on an outdoor bench alongside the salon. It seems that he had attempted to strike up conversations with certain salon customers as they came and went. After numerous clients had been rattled by the strange man, the salon owner called the police.

The cold case investigator asked the owner if she could recall just what the fellow had said to the women. She stated that her general impression was that it was more a matter of his appearance than what he might have said that actually scared the women. The investigator also asked what if anything the women he had approached might have had in common. After a bit of thought she said, "Come to think of it, all of the women were blonde."

And of course, so was Jayme Jackson.

What the salon owner said next, however, was by far of the greatest possible importance: She was certain that the day that she called the police, and the same day that the victim was also killed, was the last time she ever saw the scary-looking man on the bench. Finally, the cold case investigator asked whether or not she had told the police investigators the same account of facts immediately after the crime. The salon owner said that she had never been interviewed by anyone until the moment the cold case investigator arrived years after the crime.

A few key pieces of information had been learned:
1) A suspect whose behavior and appearance were sufficient to scare women had been lurking about up to the time of the crime.
2) The salon might have served as a place for the killer to have "scouted" potential victims.

3) The fact that he was never again seen after the crime reinforces the possibility that he might have committed the crime.
4) It appeared that the killer was fixated in some way with the victim's hair in that he had taken the time to have tied it in a knot. Thus, a salon would have been his link to his ability to feed that twisted fixation or "trigger."

---

The new investigator had both the best and worst of it: He had a strong lead to follow, however he also faced the difficult talk of attempting to identify and locate an unknown suspect. Clearly, someone in the area was likely to have known something about the stranger at the time of the crime. But it would be a seemingly impossible task to move about the immediate community asking questions about a nameless suspect years after the fact. Note the recurring nature of this problem.

The police were contacted. In a stroke of good luck, a female officer did recall the vagrant, however no official report was filed that might contain the suspect's name. He was a homeless drifter with bad hygiene, and the only other thing the officer recalled about him was that he said that he was from Iowa. He was white, age about thirty at the time, and had a pockmarked face. The new investigator spent several more days in the area of the salon seeking more information about the suspect, but none was forthcoming.

Iowa police were told about the case. They had no leads as to the suspect, however they did have information about an unsolved rape and murder in which the victim was apparently abducted from a public telephone in front of a convenient store. In that case, the victim was stabbed multiple times with an unknown type of weapon that inflicted puncture wounds.

A search was then undertaken for the suspect in shelters and other places where the homeless congregate. At each stop along the way the investigator asked about an individual who might have been reluctant to put down his knapsack or duffel bag. At perhaps the tenth stop, an elderly woman at a soup kitchen asked how in earth it was that he knew that about a fellow. She explained that only a few months earlier just such an individual attacked another homeless person for having picked up his travel bag. "Stuck him good with an ice pick, he did," she said.

As it turned out, the victim had refused to sign a complaint, however the suspect's name was on file with the local police. Thus, the hunt for Julius Wilkes was on.

Julius Wilkes Search

The prime suspect had used the name Julius Wilkes during a stay at a homeless shelter, which in no way is an actual indicator of his real name. The homeless do not generally carry identification, nor are they expected to correctly identify themselves in soup kitchens, shelters, or any other places they might come before. Thus, the cold case investigator was not expecting to be able to locate the suspect through usual means.

When searching for mainstream members of society, there are many internet-based data systems designed to locate individuals making use of a name, approximate age, and last known address. However, in order for one to be placed within such information systems, the subjects must exist within the eyes of society in general. Individuals are traced through such items as social security numbers, drivers license data, credit applications, rental and mortgage information, and many other societal trappings within which most persons travel.

However, such search tools become far less effective when the individual being sought participates in none of the above. Therefore finding individuals who fit in one of the following categories may be an extremely difficult task:

1) Long-term unemployed.
2) Certain members of the criminal community.
3) Illegal aliens.
4) Mentally handicapped individuals.

Early observations indicated that Julius Wilkes, or whoever he actually was, qualified in perhaps as many as three of the four areas listed above. Based on all of these facts the search for the murder suspect seemingly was not going to be an easy one. One might run his name for a credit check, but the report would not know the location of the tent where he would sleep that night.

When individuals travel beneath mainstream society, the only sure-fire method of locating them is to talk to people until someone is found who both knows him and is willing to tell what they know. Clearly this task would be greatly complicated by the passing of time between Jayme Jackson's murder and the onset of the cold case investigation years later.

At the outset of the cold case investigation the police denied them access to their reports. However, once it began to look like the case was the work of a serial killer, they agreed to turn their file over for inspection.

The crime scene photos showed that what had been referred to as a warm-up house also served as a locker room with two rows of benches for changing in and out of skating attire. The victim's street shoes were near where she rested in the far corner of the room. White athletic socks were pulled up high around her calves. The cold case investigator was confused by something and called the police investigator. He wanted to know where the victim's skates were, since they were not shown anywhere in the crime scene photos. He was told that they never found skates and were unsure if she actually had skated or had intended to go skating. The cold case investigator was also told that there was no indication that the victim had rented a locker as her everyday coat was found on the end of the bench not far from where she was found.

---

There were two shops in town that bought and sold used sporting goods. At the first location a crabby old lady busied herself by chain-smoking unfiltered Camels to the extent that the shop smelled like a giant ashtray. So much for clean living in the great outdoors. The cold case investigator handed her a business card.

"What are the chances that you might recall having bought a pair of lady's figure skates a couple of years ago? The seller may have been a strange type," he said.

The woman puffed on her cigarette. "You need to be on the Psychic Hotline on television since that was the craziest thing that ever happened to me," she said. "It's not every day that a woman with only one leg wants to trade in her skates."

A Police Error of Arrogance

She then went on to explain that on the day after Jayme Jackson was murdered the case was all over the media. They made it perfectly clear that she had been killed in a skating pond warm-up house. So the lady in the store told the woman to come back in an hour, that she bought things only after noon. She then called the police and told them the story that somebody possibly connected to the murder had the victim's skates. The police investigator told her that he knew that the skates were not connected to the crime.

However, when the woman returned, the storekeeper did buy the skates for $20 just because she was curious. The investigator said that he would give anything to have a look at the skates.

The lady replied that a pack of cigarettes would be plenty and that the skates were stored away in a box just in case anyone ever became interested.

The cold case investigator was told that the woman was in the habit of panhandling at the turnoff onto the state highway at the far edge of town. The shopkeeper said that the one-legged woman seemed to have left town not long after the crime.

The cold case investigator found that the woman had been replaced by a toothless fellow with snaggled white hair.

"Whatever happened to the lady with one leg who used to be out here?" said the investigator.

"Can't hear nothing," came the reply.

"But you can see . . ." the investigator said, handing the guy a $50 bill.

The panhandler snatched the money and then said that Ruby had long since lost her other leg to diabetes, and so she switched hustles. She now charged addicts to use her little shack beside the railroad yard as a place to get high. For another fifty he hopped into the investigator's car and pointed out the shack. Then minutes later the investigator returned and pounded on the front door, yelling, "Police, search warrant."

Within seconds a dozen sets of footsteps could be heard heading out the back door and into the snowy night. He then walked in the front door to see Ruby motionless in her wheelchair in the center of a front room littered with crack pipes and dirty needles. "You ain't no cop. Cops don't do warrants all alone."

He told her that it was about murder and that she could be in it or out of it, that he had the victim's figure skates that no doubt still had her prints all over them. She decided that she would be out of it since the freak that gave the skates to her meant nothing to her anyway. She said that he was a drifter who was generally pretty calm except for when he saw young suntanned blondes. Then he was likely to shake and hyperventilate. "That dude ain't wired right," Ruby said.

Ruby said that some folks call him Skittles, like the candy. Others called him some name like that. Yes, maybe Skiles. "But that's not his real name," she said. Someone who knew him from prison showed at a shelter where both Ruby and he were staying and called him some French name like "Gag-Nee." Seemingly Ruby meant that the name was Gagne, Thomas Gagne.

Ruby had not seen him since the night of the crime when he gave her the skates in return for a pack of cigarettes.

---

Prison release lists were checked and it turned out that a Thomas Gagne had been paroled to his elderly mother's home in a small college town in Iowa. The investigator went there and learned that the mother had died over two years earlier, and Gagne was on a fugitive list for having violated the terms of his parole. He had done a dozen years for stabbing a woman in the locker room of the city zoo. Although the file did not say so, the cold case investigator knew full well that the injured woman most certainly would have been blonde.

The investigator went to a college campus near where the suspect's mother had lived. A strange fellow sat on a bench watching people walk past. The investigator placed a one hundred dollar bill on the ground in front of him and kept walking. The suspect lunged for the money as the investigator grabbed the suspect's dirty duffel bag that contained a bloody ice pick, and a cheap blond wig that was tied into a knot. Unlike serial offenders with homes, this one needed to always carry his tools with him for whenever the sick urges came over him. Once the secret was out Thomas Gagne confessed to everything.

# CASE 8

## PIECING TOGETHER INFORMATION

<u>Investigative Overview</u>

Bright investigators are able to view known case facts and make sense out of what is known to be true. In this case investigators did know that the victim was mutilated; a sure sign of a crime of passion. They also noted that the victim had been attacked with a razor-sharp weapon.

Investigators learned that not very long before the crime an individual was observed in the area of the hotel where the victim was staying and was brandishing a most unusual cutting weapon. The investigators utilized the description of that individual and the described weapon as a method of tracking the suspect, eventually leading to a rapid case solution.

# CASE 8

The Crime
    Lars Janns was a Danish tourist visiting a major U.S. city. His body was found along a path beside one of the largest lakefront parks in the nation. He suffered a horizontal cut across the base of his nose, which was struck with such force that the bone was completely shattered nearly two inches deep. The same cut extended to both cheek bones and was deep enough there to make it appear as if the victim had a second set of eyelids from where the skin below the cheekbones sagged. There were large horizontal bruises across both his shins. His white designer jeans were down across his thighs, and there were no undershorts. There also was no penis nor were there testicles, at least not in place. Both had been severed and stuck side by side into the victim's mouth.

    As the lead investigator said to his partner, Lars Janns had done something to make his killer very upset indeed.

    The victim's body was discovered by an elderly couple taking their nightly stroll. They were certain that the first time they walked past what was to become a crime scene, the victim was not present, either alive or in his present condition. That had been at 8:20 p.m., dusk for that time of year. They returned along the same route and found the victim's remains at 8:48 p.m. They had seen nothing suspicious or out of the ordinary along the way.

Whatever the weapon had been, it was razor-sharp. The severed body parts were as neat and clean as if a surgeon had performed the amputation. A question as to whether more than one weapon may have been used also came into play since the wound to the face seemingly was delivered with such force. Had the attack landed on the victim's neck rather than his face, he might have been decapitated. Of course, when the issue of possible multiple weapons comes into play, so does the notion that there might have been two or more killer.

The investigators found a key for a nearby luxury hotel and went to pay it a visit. The manager said that the victim had been a guest for three days, and a variety of front desk workers all said that he came and went by himself. For the past two nights he had returned to the hotel between 2:30 and 3:00 a.m. It had been apparent that he had been drinking, but he was nothing like having been wiped-out drunk. The overnight doorman said that on both nights he had been dropped off by a Yellow Cab. On the first night he had been alone. On the next night there had been another man in the cab when he was dropped at the hotel.

There were five changes of clothes in the victim's hotel room including summer-weight sports jackets. He preferred pastel colors and Puma sports shoes. There were no undershorts to be found.

There was a personal checkbook, a Copenhagen driver's license, and a gold card case that contained gold laminated business cards that said that Lars Janns was a film producer.

Investigative Analysis

Many times investigators learn a great deal from the first hours of homicide investigation. Other times what they learn more or less acts to confirm what they thought that a case was about. Lars Janns was:

1) Killed in a mutilation murder.
2) A filmmaker from Copenhagen.
3) Was clearly humiliated – or that was the killer's intent – in the course of the crime.

Mutilation murders are often the work of male homosexual offenders. Copenhagen is often called the Pornography Capital of the World, significant in light of the victim having been a filmmaker. And the placement of the severed body parts in the victim's mouth was highly symbolic in terms of disclosing an extremely high level of rage toward Lars Janns.

An Investigative Note

In general terms, mutilation or other signs of overkill including multiple causes of death upon a victim is usually associated with the work of serial killers. However, the category of crime under current consideration, male gay upon male gay, is often quite different. Though many such crimes do involve mutilation and often severed body parts, such offenders are not usually thought to be serial killers. Where serial killers' motives for murder are typically buried, the gay offender who mutilates typically does so as a vengeful response to a perceived rejection or other type of scorn toward them on the part of the killer. Thus, whoever killed Lars Janns was not a likely serial offender.

In other instances, however, gay males may become victims of a serial killer. When such a crime pattern does surface, those killings are usually the work of an offender who is not a member of the gay community. Such serial offenders generally harbor great hatred toward gays and wish to punish them for their sexual orientation. Or in other instances the serial offender's primary motive may be monetary gain, in which instances the offender pretends to be gay himself, then lures the victim to a place where a robbery occurs. Often but not always, the victim survives. However, when such robberies upon gay men do occur, they are unlikely to report the incident to the police.

---

Early Investigation

The investigators might have started to trace taxi cabs at this point to learn exactly where the victim had spent the past two evenings, as well as to determine the identity of the man who was inside the cab that had dropped him at the hotel. However, it was decided to first learn more about the life of Lars Janns in order to learn who had taken it from him.

The investigators paid a visit to the largest gay newspaper in the city. The news editor immediately recognized the victim's name and knew of his work well. Lars Janns was the real deal. He made many films, which had won awards and played at gay festivals around the world. Though his films did explore many graphic aspects of sex, all of that was said to be on equal footing with social issues.

The victim was worth many millions, was devoted to his long-time life partner, and was scared to death of becoming HIV-positive and therefore was not one to become involved in flings.

Criminal investigation is a craft where that which is often said about homicide victims winds up being in direct contradiction to what actually killed them. Devoted husbands sneak off to ghetto alleys in order to have illicit sex with AIDS-infected prostitutes. Cub Scout leaders get their throats slit while waiting in line to buy crack cocaine.

Either a gay fellow who make films was killed because he became involved in some type of sordid or compromising situation, or it just seemed to look that way. Investigative experience dictates that there are very few coincidences.

Investigators told the news editor that they were about to search for the taxicab that drove him home. He responded by telling the investigators that he already knew where the victim had been; there had been a reception at a club in the heart of the gay community the night before. Lars was honored for his contributions to the gays, and better yet, he was hosted by Jack Collins, the only openly gay alderman in the city. The editor opened a desk drawer and handed the investigators a photo of the filmmaker and alderman about to climb into their taxi.

---

The alderman lived in a big brick bungalow on a one-way street less than a block from the lake. He answered his own doorbell and welcomed the investigators to join him in the kitchen for expresso. He had not yet heard about the crime and seemed genuinely shocked when told about what had happened.

Jack Collins told them that he had met Lars at his office at about 6 p.m. and the two of them took a taxi to the club. They had the reception at the club, which broke up about midnight, then they drank cognac with the bar owner until closing at 2 a.m. They talked about many things including the concept of a documentary film about gay elected officials. Their cab went directly from the club to the hotel, he and Lars shook hands inside the cab, and the victim got out and walked into the hotel.

At least that part of the alderman's story matched what the doorman had earlier told the investigators.

Collins told the investigators that the cabby's name was Doris Brown, also a member of the gay-lesbian community. She was something of a personal driver for the alderman who simply calls her on her cell phone whenever he needs a cab.

And so it seemed to the investigators that wherever their case was going to lead them, at least it did not seem as if they would be locking up an alderman for murder.

---

The investigators were bothered by the fact that the victim had not had a cell phone among his belongings, either on his person or in his room. They called the alderman who said that they had called each other several times and supplied the police with the number. The investigators dialed the number and as luck would have it, someone answered on the third ring.

*Investigator:*   This is the police homicide unit. Who as I talking to?

*Voice:*   Thomas Royce, sir. I found this here phone on the pier while I was fishing.

*Investigator:*   Are you at the Brooks Pier now?

*Voice:*   Catching catfish all night long. You want the phone?

The investigators arrived within ten minutes and thanked Thomas Royce for having been a good citizen. They had an evidence technician take Thomas' fingerprints so that they might be eliminated from any found on the phone. However, no other prints were found on the phone. The investigators ordered cell phone records for the six local numbers the victim had made or received, but those records would take a day to arrive. Brooks Pier was a few hundred feet from where the victim's body had been found. There was no way to know at this point how the cell phone found its way over to the pier.

A Lead

The police dispatcher told the investigators that a tactical team wanted to know their current location. Moments later a male and female tactical team pulled up alongside in their beat-up, unmarked squad car. It seems that the pair had worked the day shift in the hours before the Janns murder.

"We were working downtown all day on a robbery pattern. Just at noon there was a call right across the street from your victim's hotel. Three different calls came in that a redheaded guy dressed in camouflage was running around with a machete in his hand. By the time we got there the guy had vanished. Beat 131 took the report," the female officer said.

Her partner shifted behind the wheel. "Any chance your guy got hacked up with a weapon like that?"

The investigators looked at each other and knew they were on to something. "Here's what we have. Someone used a very big blade to put a deep slice right through the victim's nose. He also had two bad bruises across both shins, which might have come from the killer having used the blunt side of a machete. Lastly, someone performed a perfect amputation of the victim's genitals with a very sharp weapon."

The tactical girl asked, "Could the killer have used something as big as a machete on his genitals without having also hacked up the surrounding area? Do you see what I'm asking?"

The investigators nodded that they were wondering the same thing.

---

By now the investigators were in their eleventh hour on the case. They drank black coffee, then drove over to the patrol district where the beat officers who had taken the machete man report would be reporting for roll call. The officers had been assigned to a call of "man on the street with a machete." They were the first car to arrive but the offender was already gone. The first caller to 911 had been a college girl who said that the guy was early-twenties, slight of build, with carrot red haircut short. He wore Army camouflage shirt and pants, well-shined combat boots, and a huge silver machete with an orange handle. The guy was shouting that what he was going to do would be memorable. The other two callers also called from cell phones but continued on their way. They both gave similar accounts of the incident.

The investigators presented a progress report to day-shift investigators that concluded with:
1) The victim had been out both nights in town.
2) Investigators had accounted for the victim's whereabouts only for the second night.

3) The machete man on the street would be treated as the killer until proven otherwise.
4) Machete man was unlikely to have had such a weapon lying around his house at the time he became provoked.
5) Therefore, find the source of the weapon, find the suspect.

The day-shift investigators called the alderman's personal cab driver in hope that she might know where the victim had been on his first night in town. She said that she knew a driver who always waited in line for fares in front of the hotel and would find out what, if anything, he might know.

Weapon Hunt

One of the many interesting aspects of criminal investigation is that when working a case one is likely to learn about many different things. For example, when tracking a suspect who drove a sports car, investigators would speak to many individuals connected to such vehicles. Before long they would know where such cars are bought and sold, serviced, and placed on display.

In this instance the task was to learn just where one might go about buying a machete. Investigators learned that along the city's antique row were a number of shops that specialized in military memorabilia and weapons. When they opened the door of the first shop, an old-fashioned bell jingled. A little old lady sat in a huge overstuffed chair behind the counter. "I don't ever buy stolen property, detectives," she said.

The investigators laughed, explaining that they were homicide, not burglary. They inquired as to whether she might have recently sold a machete.

"I knew it, I knew it, I knew it. That guy was going to hurt somebody," she said.

She went on to explain that two days before a skinny little guy with crazed eyes came in looking to buy a machete she had on display in the window. Since she didn't like his looks she told him that it was already sold. He became upset and raised his voice at which time she reached down under the counter and came out with an antique single-action Colt .45 that she commenced to show the investigators.

"Was he on foot?" an investigator asked.

The lady shook her head. She was concerned that he might be dangerous so she went to the door and watched him walk to the end of the block where he got into a little, red, topless Jeep. She explained that there was only one other place where he might have found a machete if that was what he really wanted; GI Memories, two blocks east.

GI Memories was a dive of a place with an owner who pushed all forty of his hair strands up into a flat top. Yeah, he sold a Spanish machete to a little guy with red hair. The guy also bought some military clothing. What color was the handle? Amber, or maybe you'd call it orange. No, he had no idea what the guy's name was. No, there was nothing about the guy. The investigators were on their way out of the door when the storeowner called to them. There was one thing. As he crossed the street, he was talking to a Black chick on the street, who isn't really a chick. He/ She lives around here someplace.

Key Investigative Moments

The investigators had followed a trail of leads beautifully. They started with the theory that their suspect had bought the weapon specifically to carry out a well-planned crime. Since the victim had only been in the city for two days before his death, whatever set the killer off must have just happened – thus, his need to thereafter buy the machete. The lady in the first store thought the suspect was sufficiently deranged so that she refused to sell him the weapon. Though she was matter-of-fact about it, the lady gave them a good lead, that he drove a red Jeep. The owner of the second shop had seemingly sold him the murder weapon plus the clothing he wore while attracting attention across from the hotel earlier in the day before the crime. Perhaps the killer had been waiting for the victim to leave the hotel when witnesses called the police, thus forcing him to flee, at least for the moment. Lastly, the man in GI Memories supplied another excellent lead that the suspect knew a transvestite who lived near his store.

The investigators split up with each taking one side of the street. They canvassed the block where GI Memories was located, speaking in all to over twenty storekeepers. Three had seen a Black person dressed as a female whose actual gender might be in question. Nobody knew what she did for a living nor where she lived. The only lead that came from the canvass was that she had been seen twice in a donut shop a couple of blocks down the street.

The investigators made a call and were told that the lead investigative team had just arrived in the office. Everyone would meet at the donut shop for a briefing session. Then the old adage, "it's better to be lucky than good," came into play as a rail-thin Black person in tight white shorts and a red sequined top was standing in the doorway of the shop. They popped their police stars on her and asked her to step outside.

*Investigator:*  What's your name?

*He/She:*  Lucky Charmaign, that's my new name since conversion surgery.

*Investigator:*  From male to otherwise?

*He/She:*  You are so observant to see that I'm clearly otherwise.

*Investigator:*  We're working on the murder on the front page of the newspaper you have in your hands. Do you know who killed Lars Janns?

*He/She:*  Such a crime. He was a very pretty man. But I have no idea why I would have that kind of information.

*Investigator:*  Who's your little redheaded buddy with the red Jeep?

*He/She:*  My, but we do come prepared now don't we? You are talking about Jamie Sprinkles.

| | |
|---|---|
| *Investigator:* | Is Jamie his real name or is it like Lucky Charmaign? |
| *He/She:* | That's the name I know him by, but why don't you just ask him yourself? He works at the soft-serve ice cream stand right across the street. His Jeep is usually parked on the side street. |

---

Moments later the two teams of investigators saw the red Jeep, ran the plate, and learned that it was registered to James Jon Sprinkles, with a residence address only a few blocks away. One team covered the back door to the ice cream shop while the lead team went inside. They pulled their stars and said "You got to come with us." Without as much as a word, Jamie hung up his apron and told an older woman behind the counter that he was going off duty for the day. He marched right past the investigators and through the door. After a frisk for weapons, handcuffs were placed on behind his back and they were off to investigative headquarters.

Sorting Things Out

Investigators had a suspect in custody. One of the most interesting aspects of criminal investigation is that one can never predict which suspects will readily confess, which ones need to be convinced that telling the truth is always a good idea, and which ones will invoke their Miranda rights and say nothing. Sound custodial interrogation is based on the interrogator explaining precisely how the suspect has been linked to the crime, then asking the suspect to provide a reasonable explanation as to why he/she became a suspect. In turn, the investigator then breaks down the suspect's attempt at a logical explanation by pointing out that which is actually illogical.

In this instance the lead investigators explained the following facts to Jamie Sprinkles.

1) A noted filmmaker from Copenhagen was killed in a city park near the lakefront.

2) The murder weapon was an oversized cutting tool.

3) The killer had displayed extreme rage in having carried out the crime.

4) Earlier the same day a young redheaded fellow was seen waving a machete on the street across from the victim's hotel.

5) Witnesses to that act would soon be arriving at investigative headquarters to view Jamie in a line-up.

6) Investigators had traced the purchase of a machete to GI Memories where the owner stated that he sold such a weapon to a young redheaded fellow.

7) He would soon by viewing Jamie in another line-up.

8) Investigators were in the process of gaining a search warrant for Jamie's Jeep and apartment seeking the machete or other items attached to the crime.

9) The results of those investigative steps will either implicate or exonerate Jamie as the killer.

---

The investigators drank cans of diet soda and Jamie had black coffee.

*Investigator:* Would you like to tell us how you knew Lars Janns?

*Jamie:* Who said I knew him? I never said that.

*Investigator:* Given a little time we'll find the answer to that question. You want my best guesses?

*Jamie:* Why not . . .?

*Investigator:* Jamie, you're good looking enough to have been featured in one of Lars' movies. Either you contacted him or he ran into you. Either way the topic would have been the same, Jamie in the movies. Except something went very wrong. Did he break a promise to you, Jamie?

---

Jamie Sprinkles' eyes began to well up. He looked emotionally ready to unload and tell the story.

The investigator went on. "The way I figure it, Lars told you that you were in on a movie project, then he behaved cruelly toward you in some way. So what happened?"

Jamie was ready to burst.

The investigator continued, "Just tell us what happened. All of us know that those witnesses are going to pick you out of the line-ups."

Jamie told the story. He had followed an entertainment blog that told about the filmmaker's U.S. trip. Jamie learned which hotel Lars was going to be staying at, and waited until he arrived. He approached him outside the hotel lobby and asked if they could talk. Lars told him he was far too cute not to get to know. So that evening they had a drink at the bar of another hotel on the next block. Before long Lars told Jamie that he would feature him in whatever his next film was to be. There was then a bit of rubbing one another in a booth in the bar. It was then that the victim-to-be told Jamie that he was insufficiently endowed to take his clothes off before a camera. Then Lars laughed at him and walked off into the night.

"So you can see why I had to kill him," Jamie said.

The search warrant turned up a bloody shirt in the wayback of the Jeep that had a mixture of the blood types of both victim and killer. Jamie led investigators to a hidden cove near the fishing pier where he tossed the machete into the water. Police divers recovered it soon after. Jamie said he had no idea as to how the victim's cell phone found its way to the pier where it was found.

Jamie Sprinkles entered a plea of guilty to first degree murder and was sentenced to 200 years in prison.

# CASE 9

## WORKING OLD AND COLD CASES

Investigative Overview

In many long-time unsolved murders the case is classified as "Known but Blown," meaning that the police are certain they know the identity of the wanted offender, but that the killer has either fled the jurisdiction, or the police are simply unable to prove their case. In other instances, the case may have been unsolved because of poor luck or bad timing. Perhaps an eyewitness may have been standing near the crime scene but left an instant before the police arrived. In fewer cases the police may have simply failed to conduct an adequate criminal investigation.

In the following case it appears that the crime should not have been too hard to solve had the police been sufficiently interested; however, it seems as if the investigators did not try too hard. The 15-year-old victim drank and smoked marijuana and likely was seen as being less than an innocent victim.

The benefit of working such cold cases is that everything often remains untouched and in place, thus the case solution even decades later is often quite easily accomplished.

# CASE 9

The Case

A civilian cold case investigator was contacted by a woman named Betty Crawford, who claimed that a major city police department had failed to act on her information concerning the death of her best friend more than thirty-five years before. Penny Hutson was stomped and beaten to death on her fifteenth birthday.

The victim and her friend lived in a working-class suburb near a major city. The year was 1972. The two girls were old for their age, drinking and smoking marijuana, all of this during the middle of the hippie generation. They were part of a youth movement in the community where scores and often hundreds of young people gathered at a local forest preserve to visit and invariably get high.

There was not a whole lot of parental supervision in many of the kids' lives. The victim's fifteenth birthday fell on a Tuesday night, yet she and Betty had their choice of two different parties to attend. Their first stop was at the apartment of two guys in their early twenties, where beer, whiskey, and pot were served. People came and went over the course of the night. At about 10 p.m. Betty told Penny that she was leaving for the other party not far away. None of this posed any sort of problem for Penny as she only lived two blocks away, and she said she planned on walking home before very long. A woman named Wendy Winn, who was a single mother, lived upstairs of where the party was being held. Penny frequently babysat for her kids, so Wendy popped in and out of the party that night to talk to Penny and the others and have a quick beer. Partygoers would later say that the party ended at about 1 a.m. That would turn out to be the last time any of them would ever see the birthday kid alive again.

The Crime

At about 2:30 a.m. neighbors in a quiet inner-city neighborhood of the major city would report having heard noises coming from an alley near a major intersection. The disturbance in the alley went on for long enough for three residents to walk out into their respective backyards to see just what was going on.

What at least two of them saw was a blue 1963 or 64 Chevy parked in the alley with its motor running. Its driver's side door was open. A light-haired, lean, young, White person was some twenty feet to the rear of the car, repeatedly stomping on a young girl lying prone on the ground. She could be heard whimpering as the attack continued. One of the witnesses was brave enough to move from his rear gate and into the alley. The attacker responded to this by jumping into the car and backing it up toward where the witness was positioned. He would later state that in the process the attacker nearly ran over the victim still on the ground. At least two of the witnesses ran inside to call the police. When they arrived they found that the victim was still breathing. She was kept alive for four days, never regaining consciousness, and died of a fractured skull and brain damage. Penny Hutson passed away four days after having turned fifteen years old.

Early Investigation

The major city investigators were alleged to have been slow in starting their inquiries. Most individuals would say decades later that the police never investigated anything whatsoever in the four days between the attack on Penny Hutson and her death four days later. Once the word spread of her death among the youths at the forest preserve, they discussed how they expected to be questioned, but most of them never were.

However, the victim's friend Betty became relentless in her own fact-finding. She quickly learned that Penny had left the party with an older guy named Damien Dillon. Dillon had a bad reputation for mistreating girls to the extent that more than one of those at the party cautioned the victim about going anywhere with him. She had replied that she was only going to get a ride home with him. Damien Dillon was often in the company of a fellow named Wesley Dillon. The pair was generally thought to be cousins.

Several of the victim's girlfriends contacted the police to tell them about Damien Dillon. Investigators responded by making comments to the effect that Penny Hutson was a slut. As outrageous as such a statement might have been, it actually made sense on two levels.

Recall that the crime in question occurred in 1972, only four years after major riots in many cities between anti-war "hippie" protestors and the police. Thus anyone who dressed like a hippie and smoked dope was seen by most police officers as the enemy. Secondly, within many police circles the quality and depth of homicide investigations are often determined by the degree to which the police see the victim as having been innocent. Since the dead little girl smoked and drank, she apparently was seen as anything but an innocent victim.

Betty Crawford's initial belief about Damien Dillon turned tragic when the following summer she was at the forest preserve on an evening when perhaps several hundred young people were present, drinking and drugging. Betty knew Wesley Dillon by sight but had no idea of his name, so when he offered her a ride home she had no reason to be concerned.

She was led to a black car where a blond guy was waiting behind the wheel. She and Wesley got into the car, and she began directing them toward her house. As they neared her home the driver said to Wesley, "This is right where Hutson lived." Betty then confronted him stating that he must be Damien Dillon. Both men then began striking her with their fists. They then pulled the car over in a darkened area where both sexually attacked her. The attackers discussed how they killed Penny during the course of raping Betty, before throwing her out of the car.

Betty Crawford called the local suburban police who acted disinterested in what she had to say. One of the officers told her that she got just what she deserved for drinking, drugging, and generally having been a slut. She was never contacted by investigators, thus a rape offense was disregarded perhaps again because the victim was not seen as having been innocent.

Some cold case investigations are so deep and complex that finding a positive resolution may actually take years rather than weeks or months. However, every once in a while a case comes along where very little investigation is actually required simply because of how little the police investigators did in the aftermath of the crime.

Gathering Information

One of the primary principles of cold case investigation is that the task of arriving at case solution is a far more difficult task when investigators do not have access to the initial police reports. In this instance there was no percentage in the civilian investigators to alert the authorities that a new investigation was underway. Nobody greatly enjoys others fixing their past failures, especially within a forum as public as old murder cases. Perhaps hard feelings between the police and cold case investigators were inevitable in the long run, however that was simple conjecture as to what might later occur.

Betty Crawford, the victim's brother, and a few other supporters of the cause created a website, "Justice for Penny." Front-page center was the description of the killer and his car. There was also a list of three alleged witnesses to the crime:

Frederick Baroni

Jesus Delgado

Madison Mendrick

The website stated that police investigators had said over a period of decades that their ability to investigate the murder was being held up by their collective inability to locate the witnesses. At first glance that made little sense since major city police departments have access to the finest private access information sources possible. At the push of a button they might tap into Department of Motor Vehicle records as to drivers' licenses, autos registered to individuals, and past driving record transcripts. Social Security Administration records, property tax statements, public utility records, and scores of other sources were at the disposal of the police investigators.

What was hard to understand was the apparent reluctance of the police investigators to open a cold case investigation in the years that followed. There were two possible reasons for their apparent interest in keeping an apparently solvable case buried, but neither of them made much sense. One possibility was that they were concerned that if they reopened the Hutson case, it would come out that the initial investigators had blown the case off. The second thought was that the police simply did not see Betty Crawford as being credible, so that her indictment of the two alleged offenders was incorrect.

<u>Witness Search</u>

Although civilian investigators are at a great disadvantage in terms of information sources, there are many excellent Internet search sites. Most do charge an annual fee although many do supply at least a limited amount of information without charge, an inducement for researchers to pay the fee in order to gain as much information as possible. The basic information required to run a successful name check is first and last name, last known state of residence, and hopefully an approximate age of the subject.

Though one does not always get a direct lead as to all the identifiers submitted, very often there are enough individuals with the same last name that investigators have a starting point to begin a search. Other individuals in the state searched with the same last name as the subject are often relatives. Certain search sources also provide free lists of possible relatives of the subject. Investigators may then cross-reference the relatives' names thereby creating a full file of possible family members. Even when one runs highly unusual last names there are nearly always individuals with that name listed in the data bank.

However, such was not the case over the early stages of the search for two of the alleged missing witnesses. There were no matches under the name Baroni and Mendrick. After several hours of searching and attempts at nationwide searches, the cold case investigator began experimenting with variations in spelling. By using the spelling

"Barone" rather than the spelling supplied with an "i" at the end of the name, a Frederick Barone was found in the search tool. However, if the subject were still alive, he would have been ninety-eight years old. His name was then searched for relatives, and a nephew in another state was located and contacted.

He stated that Frederick Barone had died in 1989 and that as a youth he had overheard his uncle recounting the attack upon Penny Hutson. He had lived on the block where the crime had taken place, and he had walked out into his yard to investigate the cause of the noise. He also said that he had given his name to the police that night but that nobody ever contacted him again about what he may have seen.

The search for Madison Mendrick went almost exactly the same way as with Barone. Nothing came up on the subject until the spelling variation of "Menderick" was used. This potential witness had died in about 1993, and family members did not recall his having talked about the incident.

The search for the last witness, Jesus Delgado, was complicated by the fact that there were more than a hundred subjects in the area with that name. Even after limiting the search to older individuals, the possible list still had more than thirty names. Each such subject was searched for and contacted when possible, however he could not be found.

---

The search for Delgado and other potential witnesses shifted. Many public libraries have a reference source variously called a reverse directory or criss-cross directory. Rather than categorizing individuals by name, information is listed by address. Turn to an address and you get the name of whoever lives there along with their listed phone number. In the Hutson case the search for a 1972 edition of a reverse directory was a difficult process, which eventually led to the investigator contacting the book publisher.

It was now possible to learn the name of everyone who lived on either side of the alley where the murder took place. Two city blocks of residents included more than fifty names. A current issue of the reverse directory was obtained and compared to the 1972 version. Only three last names were in common over the three-plus decade passing of time. One of those names was Morales. Omar Morales was contacted and stated that he still lived in the same house in which he was raised. He recalled his late mother talking about the crime and the fact that their neighbor Jesus Delgado had confronted the killer in the alley and was nearly run over by the killer's car. Jesus had also said that the killer called to someone inside the car during the incident and that a male voice came from within the offender's car. This was a turning point in the sense that it was the first time that an accomplice had been implicated in the crime.

Omar Morales said that Delgado had retired to Puerto Vallarta, Mexico, at least twenty years ago. If still alive, he would now be about ninety years old. Another name present in both directories was a Mildred Simpson, who lived on the street on the other side of the alley from Omar Morales. Mildred knew nothing about the crime, but she did have a phone number for Yesenia Delgado, wife of Jesus. The third name that remained on the block for all of those years had passed away earlier in the year. The cold case investigator contacted the Delgados in Mexico. Jesus told the story of the crime as if it had taken place the day before. He had heard a garbage can being knocked over in the alley, then a scream followed by sobbing, then a car door slamming. As he moved toward the alley, he saw a tall, thin, blond guy about twenty bracing himself between two garbage cans then pouncing on a tiny female figure prone on the ground in the alley. As he walked into the alley, he screamed at the attacker to leave the victim alone. The attacker called to someone inside the car, then ran and jumped into the car. He then backed up as if intending to run over Delgado, but in the process just missed running over Penny Hutson. Jesus ran inside and called the police, then told his story to several different police officers and investigators. However, nobody ever followed up to interview him after the time of the attack. He said that the offender's car was a dark blue, early-sixties, Chevy two-door.

What Was Accomplished

The task of locating the three possible witnesses, which the police had said held up their

214

ability to work the investigation, had taken a lone civilian investigator one full day's work without any access to police data sources. What those questioned said had reinforced the commonly held version of events. However, the passing of thirty-five years can complicate a murder investigation in a thousand ways. For example, had the police developed a suspect within a year or so of the murder, they might have expected that all three witnesses would be able to identify the killer, first in a photo gallery, and then later in a police line-up. However, two of the witnesses had taken what they saw to their graves with them, and it would be futile to ask Jesus Delgado to try to identify a suspect between fifty-five and sixty years of age for a crime that had taken place when he was perhaps in his early-twenties.

Although not a great deal of information gathered by the cold case investigator would actually advance the investigation, what was singularly important was the fact that everything that was learned fit the general theory that Damien Dillon remained a prime suspect in the murder of Penny Hutson.

---

The cold case investigator searched for Wendy Winn, the woman who lived in the building where Penny had attended her last party. She was tracked to a tiny farming community where she had lived for decades. She said that one of the reasons she kept walking in on the party was that she was extremely concerned that Penny was with a light-haired guy named Dillon who had a very bad reputation for beating girls. She said that at about 1 a.m. she walked back in as the party was breaking up and Penny and Dillon were not there. She looked out a window overlooking the street and saw the two of them standing alongside a blue Chevy, which she had seen Dillon driving in the past. When asked about whether she had seen any other males outside with the victim and suspect, she said no.

Thus at the completion of the second day of the cold case investigation the following evidence had been gathered:

1) Wendy Winn was able to place the victim in the company of Damien Dillon at the party.

2) Ms. Winn also saw them standing alongside a blue Chevy after the party broke up.

3) The victim had said that Damien Dillon was going to drive her home after the party.

4) Jesus Delgado placed an offender stomping the victim. He fit the known description of Damien Dillon and placed a blue Chevy at the crime scene.

5) Others told Betty Crawford that the victim had left the party with Damien Dillon.

6) Several months later Betty confronted Damien and Wesley Dillon as to their involvement in the crime. Both responded by attacking her both sexually and physically.

Thus the makings of a strong circumstantial case was forming against Damien Dillon, if not against both suspects.

## Hunt for Suspects

Whenever multiple suspects are linked to a case, the plan should always be that the less involved individual should be dealt with first. Many serious crimes are solved by getting accomplices to turn on one another. One great interrogation room inducement is to persuade less accountable offenders to testify against the more accountable. Thus the actual shooter in a robbery-murder becomes a more highly prized conviction than is the getaway driver who never left the car while the crime was carried out. In virtually all states Felony Murder laws state that all involved in the commission of a felony offense become legally responsible for resulting deaths. Therefore the strategy is to point out to the less-involved offender that he might not have had any idea of what his partner was doing inside the crime scene. As such, if he links the actual shooter to the crime and becomes willing to testify to it in court, he is likely to receive a less serious sentence based on a plea-bargaining agreement brokered by the police interrogator and later approved by the prosecutor's office.

In the Penny Hutson case all information would indicate that Wesley Dillon was present at the time of the murder. This theory comes from two pieces of collected evidence: Jesus Delgado overheard the actual killer speaking to someone inside the car, then heard a voice from within respond; and more importantly, Betty Crawford stated that both Damien and Wesley Dillon discussed having killed Penny while attacking Crawford.

To the extent that the above case facts involving the suspects are accurate, Wesley Dillon rode in the car with Damien and the victim from the suburbs to the inner city where the stomping in the alley occurred. Based on the crime inflicted on Betty Crawford, it is reasonable to assume that both men attempted to engage Penny in sexual conduct; and when she refused, she was attacked inside the car. Then Damien drove into the alley with the intent to kill her and leave her in the alley, thus distancing himself from the crime as much as possible. However, his plan became flawed by the fact that witnesses overheard the noises in the alley and saw both the killer and his auto.

---

Wesley Dillon had lived in a suburb not far from where both Penny and Betty lived. It was thought that he had attended the local public high school and was perhaps nearing twenty at the time of the crime. He would therefore be near age sixty now. His name was run in a variety of sequences on the same search sites as used to locate the missing witnesses. Based on lists of possible relatives the name Tina Dillon surfaced. In turn, her name was run through the same process. Research indicated that her maiden name had apparently been Keefer.

Then she became Tina Dillon, then finally it seemed as if the same individual once again changed her name to Tina Armstrong.

At that point she seemed to have vanished, at least from the part of the country where the crime and subsequent investigation were centered. The same data was checked on a state-by-state basis, which resulted in a possible location of an individual by that name living in a tiny town in rural West Virginia. It was learned that this party was married to Oren Armstrong, who fortunately had a listed phone number.

Tina Armstrong answered the phone and confirmed that she had once been married to Wesley Dillon. The cold case investigator told her only that Wesley's name had come up along with a Damien Dillon as having been involved in an attack incident many years ago.

Tina gave the following statements:

1) She had been married to Wesley for a decade and had a grown child with him.
2) She had never known him to exhibit violent behavior.
3) She had never heard of Damien Dillon and did not think he was a relative.
4) She had no idea how to contact Wesley.

The Psychology of Cold Case Investigation

Very few crafts are as clearly defined as is criminal investigation. When homicide investigators succeed, killers are removed from the general population and they are unable to kill again. By contrast, failed investigations lead to killers being able not only to repeat their performances but it also enables them to become more and more confident with the passing of each day that they have successfully eluded detection.

When offenders kill and remain free, they become a little less concerned about being caught with the passing of time until eventually the worry leaves them. The worry is often eventually replaced with an arrogance based on their perceived cleverness at having defeated the criminal justice system. The time comes when they no longer fear the appearance of strangers at their door or a strange number on the telephone called id.

Therefore, it is not hard to imagine just how Wesley Dillon must have felt when his former wife called to say that someone was looking for him in conjunction with an old "attack" of some kind. Thus it was not surprising when Wesley Dillon could not resist immediately calling the cold case investigator to learn whether his long since forgotten worst fear had surfaced more than thirty-five years after the crime.

*Wesley:* I heard you were looking for me. I don't know anything about a murder.

*Investigator:* I never said anything about a murder, but thank you for calling.

*Wesley:* So what's this about?

*Investigator:* Someone asked me to look into an attack on a woman thirty-five years ago. Your name came up in conjunction with the incident. Do

|              | you know someone named Damien Dillon? |
|:-------------|:--------------------------------------|
| *Wesley:*    | He was a hoodlum from the neighborhood where I grew up. But I never even talked to him. |
| *Investigator:* | You might clear yourself simply by providing us with an old picture of you. The witness might say that she must have been thinking of someone else. You could be out of this just that quickly. |

Wesley said that he would gladly send the investigator his high school graduation photo to show the witness. He also asked who the witness was but was quickly told that such information was not about to be divulged.

---

The following day an attorney called the cold case investigator stating that he had been retained by Wesley Dillon, therefore further contact with the suspect would not be permitted. The attorney was told that police investigators would no doubt be pleased to know that.

Even though Damien Dillon had yet to be searched for, the call from Wesley Dillon made it important to notify police investigators of recent developments. The call brought about three important issues: The first was how quickly Wesley had called the cold case investigator after having been contacted by his former wife. The second was that he had slipped on the phone by having mentioned murder. Guilty knowledge does things like that. The third issue was that Wesley must have been panicked to have retained counsel as quickly as he had.

Wesley Dillon was emotionally on the run. It was therefore extremely important to track exactly with whom he made telephone contact from the moment that he learned from his former wife that he was under investigation. Very often accomplices in serious crimes maintain in touch with one another for reasons just like what was now taking place. Once one suspect learns of problems, he is likely to reach out to his accomplice to get his take on conditions. Similarly, Wesley may have also confided in other friends or family about the offense in the past. If so, he would likely call such persons for counsel or advice.

In such instances it is important to gain all possible phone records in order to locate possible information sources or even the second killer. Since civilian investigators have no authority to gain criminal subpoenas for such seizures, it would have to become the work of police investigators.

Betty Crawford contacted the police and talked to the investigator who had recently told her that nothing could be done until the witnesses were located. She gave him the status of the witnesses located, as well as the account of how Wesley Dillon had seemingly incriminated himself before the cold case investigator.

Rather than to be heartened by the investigative progress, the police were highly upset that a civilian investigator had made contact with a murder suspect. Betty pointed out that the police had failed to do any of that over the previous one-third of a century.

The police investigator had hostile words for the cold case investigator who correctly mentioned that he had not made contact at all with the suspect. Rather, he had located his former wife who in turn had contacted the suspect. In turn, Wesley Dillon initiated contact with the cold case investigator. Regardless of the semantics, the bottom line was that the above-described activities initiated by the cold case investigator forced the hands of the police so that they could no longer ignore the Penny Hutson case.

---

Damien Dillon Search

Betty Crawford's initial information about the suspects was to the effect that they were supposed to have been cousins and that Damien Dillon was originally from Florida. His name was associated with a John and Germaine Dillon, from the same town as the victim. That address was visited, and an elderly neighbor told the cold case investigator that the parents had moved to a rural Midwestern city in the late 1970s. An Internet source disclosed that a John Dillon had lived at an address in that town. Public library records in that town were researched, which disclosed that Damien Dillon had been arrested numerous times on possession of drugs charges and had served two prison sentences. Then in 1982 he was sought by the local police for having beaten and sexually attacked a young woman.

Damien Dillon fled the area before he could be arrested on those charges, however only months later he was arrested on a felony weapons charge in Florida at which time the arrest warrant for the battery and sex charges surfaced. He did time in a Florida prison for the weapons charge, then had been extradited on the sex case. He was convicted and did a decade in prison for that case.

Over the next decades Damien Dillon spent most of his time being arrested for drug charges and getting married at least ten times. After sifting through piles of county documents, it seemed sure that there were several more marriages than divorces. This was vitally important information in the sense that the combination of former wives and drug use might turn out to be lethal for the suspect. In many instances former spouses have many strong motives for telling what they know about their former mates. Add that concept to the fact that drug addicts are often given to talking too much about sensitive issues while under the influence. Based on this proposition, it was reasonable to think that at least one of Damien Dillon's ex-wives might well have been told about his having killed Penny Hutson.

Over the next two days more than thirty Florida addresses were associated with the suspect.

It was then possible to establish which of the wives had lived at each location. Next, current addresses for each of the ten wives, past and present, were learned. Finally, what seemed to be a current address for the suspect was determined. A contact in Florida visited that address and confirmed his presence there.

All of this material gathered by the cold case investigator was turned over to the police.

Cleared Exceptionally and Closed

The police investigators did check Wesley Dillon's phone records and found that he had made a series of calls to Florida until he located Damien and told him about the cold case investigation.

When confronted with that information, Wesley Dillon admitted to having been present inside the car when Damien attempted to have sex with Penny Hutson. At first she told him to stop, then she screamed and fought Damien's sexual advances, punching him in his groin in the process. Damien then pulled into the alley and bodily tossed the victim from the car and onto the ground, where he then repeatedly stomped her about the head and body. Wesley stated that he was too afraid to come forward and tell what had happened, but now he would be more than happy to tell about what had happened in court in the interest of saving himself from death row. Thus the prosecutors made the decision not to charge Wesley in the case in return for his testimony.

The police then obtained an arrest warrant charging Damien Dillon with the murder of Penny

Hutson. Police investigators then flew to Florida to personally make the arrest. They confirmed that the suspect was indeed at the address supplied them by the cold case investigation. They knocked on the suspect's front door while local officers covered the back door. Then a single shot rang out, after which the police knocked down the suspect's door. They found him resting on the edge of a chair with a revolver in his hand and a bullet hole in his head where he shot himself. Thus the Penny Hutson case was cleared thirty-six years and ten months after she was murdered.

The police case classification "Cleared Exceptionally" indicates that the police know where the offender is located but cannot charge him criminally due to certain circumstances.

What If . . .

Betty Crawford and the victim's brother, Jim, felt as if their efforts to solve Penny's case had been ignored by an entire generation of police investigators. Whether or not their perception of events was accurate, what seems certain is that once Wesley Dillon contacted the cold case investigator and acted guilty in a variety of ways, the police were essentially left with no choice except to work the case. Apart from the role of the police, the fact is that the entire cold case investigation was accomplished over one four-day period. Any other discussion of what the police may or may not have done is immaterial. The murder of a girl on her fifteenth birthday was cleared, better very late than never.

# CASE 10

# MATCHING INTELLIGENCE
# WITH KILLERS

Investigative Overview

Certain members of the criminal community see themselves as being above detection. The infamous acts of serial offenders demonstrate this point of view. Often the brightest of criminals taunt the police by their actions. First, they may take an extraordinary amount of time in the commission of their crimes, apparently ignoring concerns of being discovered in the act of the crime. Secondly, notable serial offenders have been known to write letters to the police and media announcing their next intended act.

In all such situations offenders who see themselves as intellectually superior to others seem to take great joy in "outsmarting" the authorities. In this case the investigator faced having to solve a murder apparently committed among a group of noted geniuses. Yet he did solve the case through common sense analysis of the known case facts, proving no one is too smart to get away with murder.

# CASE 10

The Crime

Bradley Ward was a supposed advertising creative genius who was a part of a most non-traditional ad firm. A former university professor named Maxine Roxie gathered five of her brightest students and opened an agency, which served the hip-hop culture market. Their best known work was a campaign for an athletic shoe company in which the television commercial depicted a series of youths making good their getaways from having committed purse snatchings, robberies, and other street crimes. The advertisements resulted in overnight success for the shoe company, creative awards within the industry, and protest marches on the part of the police and conservative church groups.

The victim was found in his large corner office spread out across the bench press he had been working on during his lunch hour. His forehead was caved in where the barbell came crashing down on him. The office was littered with broken pencils, ripped apart erasers, and snapped paper clips. Members of the firm had explained to the police that Ward compulsively destroyed office supplies as he brainstormed. Their investigation ruled that Bradley Ward's death was accidental as he lost his grip on the barbell as he held it above his head.

Maxine Roxie called on a private investigator to explain that each of her surviving employees loathed the victim for excellent reasons and that she did not believe in coincidences, thus one of them must have killed him. She went over her list of suspects:

Pierre Tewksbury was an openly gay princess who was madly in love with the victim, but all he got in return were horrible ongoing taunts.

Gina Nolan was a beautiful Black woman who had been engaged to marry a major league baseball player until the handsome victim stepped in and stole her away. Then a week after she broke up with her fiancée Ward laughed in her face and told her that it had just been a challenge and he had never had a real interest in her.

Wanda Filipek was married to a heroin addict and went away with him while he was in rehab. Ward knew that she had been sleeping with Dan Ricketts, the last of the firm's employees. While Wanda was gone the victim took Ricketts aside and told him in apparent confidentiality that Wanda went away to die from full-blown Aids. Ricketts, of course, then believed that he too was destined to die since he had been Wanda's lover. By the time Wanda returned, Ricketts had lost twenty pounds and his hair had fallen out in clumps.

Wanda Filipek also had a motive of her own in that when she walked back into the office, Dan Ricketts had something of a meltdown during the course of which their affair came to the surface. News of the extramarital relationship caused her husband to once again relapse on heroin. All in all any one of his co-workers might have done Ward in.

---

The investigator called for a meeting at the agency office with all of the surviving employees present. All appeared as requested but none were happy about it. The general feeling was that the victim had been evil enough to plan his own death just to make the agency staff suspect.

Pierre Tewksbury was especially hostile toward the investigator. "You might not realize that each of us are recognized geniuses. That's the very premise for this agency. Therefore if any one of us had killed Bradley, you would be in way over your head in terms of proving your case." While he was making his statement, Pierre pointed a tiny finger toward the investigator. His wrist was limp and had a thin green rubberband around it.

The investigator was calm as could be. "I'm not here to convince you that I'm bright. I'd just like to earn my fee by learning whether or not somebody killed Bradley Ward."

Gina Nolan smiled and showed a quick mind, stating that it was not like the victim had been killed in a city park. Since he was found dead in their office, if he was murdered it was implicit that one of them committed the crime. Only Maxine Roxie had not been in the office at the time of the death.

Once they got down to questioning, it was established that between noon and 1 p.m. each of them had stopped by the open door to talk to Ward about one thing or another. Each was seen standing by the door by at least one of the others, but none of them had gone inside as far as anyone knew.

Dan Ricketts seemed far less hostile to the investigator than the others did. He matter-of-factly inquired of the investigator whether he had considered just how a killing might have been accomplished. The investigator replied that so far his best theory was that someone tickled Bradley, which forced him to lose control of the barbell, which then smashed his forehead. Wanda Filipek endorsed that theory, but only one of them had the wingspan of a pro basketball player who might have administered the tickle while standing in the doorway to the victim's office.

Making Sense of Facts

The investigator went back for another look at the photos of Bradley Ward lying across the weight bench. As one looked into his office from the doorway, his head was at the left and his feet to the right. The bench had a stand where the barbell was to be replaced once the lifting set was completed, but the victim died because he was unable to get the weight back onto the stand.

After the barbell came crashing down atop his head, the barbell tumbled to the right. Its handle was covered with blood indicating that the bar had made contact with Ward's forehead just to the right of center. There were two 25-pound plates on each side of the bar. That was an even hundred pounds, and the bar itself was another thirty-five pounds. Bradley Ward was a big strong-looking fellow who should have been able to press far more than the amount he was working with when he met his death.

Therefore, the investigation centered on just how an individual, who lifts weights often enough to have all that equipment in his office, could have dropped such a relatively light amount of weight onto his own head. Add the second element that he died in an office where everyone there had his/her own reason for wishing him dead.

Upon thumbing through the death scene photos for yet another time, the investigator noticed that on Ward's right cheek, alongside where blood had run down from his head and down onto his face, was something that looked not unlike a bee sting. It was pinkish in color and raised and slightly swollen. This photo was then compared with later photos taken at the medical examiner's office in which the mark in question was far less distinct and might easily have gone unobserved if someone were not actually looking for it.

---

Maxine Roxie called the investigator to report that Wanda Filipek had not shown up for work on the morning following the staff having met with the investigator. She was not answering either her cell or house phone. Maxine had taken a taxi over to the brownstone where Wanda lived, as she needed her animation for a new project meeting with a client. Both her car and her husband's truck were gone. Maxine Roxie's question to the investigator was whether Wanda's sudden disappearance meant that she was the guilty party. His response was that speculation was generally a waste of time.

Investigative Analysis

A great deal of crime solution stems from one's ability to make sense out of what the crime scene is trying to say. Many times the most obvious clues are the ones that are most difficult to see. For example, one of the cleverest places to hide drugs was inside a bag of Hershey's Kisses candy sitting atop a kitchen counter in plain view. After having searched everywhere else, a narcotics officer asked the smug lady of the house if he might have a piece of candy. She immediately gave up her cause and asked how he could have possibly known what she had done. So he explained:

"I knew that the heroin was in the apartment and it wasn't anywhere else, so it had to be here. So what you must have done was opened each tinfoil wrapped piece of candy, taken out the candy, replaced it with the heroin, and then carefully closed the foil back up." And of course, that was precisely what the lady dealer had done. She had operated on the premise that the police would overlook the most obvious place to hide her dope bag.

And now the investigator knew exactly how Bradley had been "tickled" while lifting weights.

The advertising staff was once again gathered, but this time at the investigator's office where they were also joined by a team of homicide investigators. Everyone was present including the previously missing Wanda Filipek, who had been busy getting her husband back into a rehab facility.

The investigator and Maxine Roxie sat at a large desk in the front of the office. The agency employees sat in a semi-circle of chairs across from them at the table, and two female homicide investigators had situated themselves between the various suspects and the door just in case any heavy work needed to be done.

The investigator began with the following announcement:

There were two parts to the murder weapon, and yes, it was murder. One part was a projectile that was found at the death scene, which is now officially a murder scene. The second part of the weapon stayed with the killer, and I believe that it remains with him at this moment. The investigator allowed his eyes to roam across the desk as the agency folks all stared back and forth at one another. Everyone was talking at once, but it did not yet seem anyone among the collection of self-professed geniuses had figured out how the crime had been committed.

"Mr. Tewksbury, have you a theory as to the method of the crime?" asked the investigator.

"I really think that you're talking nonsense, is what I think," said Tewksbury.

The investigator said that he would be more direct, and then went ahead. "It was possible to extract DNA from the projectile. It had a trace of Bradley Ward's blood on it in one part, and an unknown donor's DNA elsewhere. The police have been granted a court order to take a blood sample from each of you if it comes to that."

Gina Nolan asked how the police allowed the killer to walk in with the murder weapon still in his/her possession. The investigator said that in its current state that portion was relatively harmless, much like an unloaded gun. Gina then asked how it was possible for the murder projectile to have been present at the crime scene without having been previously detected.

One of the homicide investigators asked if they might wrap this up so that they could cuff the killer and be on their way to the station.

The crime was then explained by the investigator. The floor of Ward's office was littered with broken office supplies, pencils and paper clips included. Each of the employees had stopped by the victim's office, standing in the doorway while Ward lifted, but each worker could vouch for the next that nobody went inside at any time. So the question was, how was he "tickled" into dropping the barbell onto his head?

Somebody took a paper clip, which he/she had broken in half so that it was a horseshoe-shaped metal. The killer knew that if the plan went well, the broken paper clip would simply come to rest alongside the many others that the victim himself had broken earlier.

Pierre Tewksbury interrupted to say that no thrown half paper clip could have injured or distracted the victim. The investigator agreed but explained that a sling-shot-like device had been used to send the paper clip sailing forward at many miles per hour.

It was then that Maxine Roxie became the first of the geniuses to figure it out. That little wimp Pierre used the rubberband that he always wears around his wrist to shoot Bradley with the paper clip. When it struck him, Bradley Ward was momentarily startled and dropped the barbell onto his own forehead.

The female homicide investigators told Pierre to stand up, which he did on very shaky legs. Then the gay genius made one of the dumbest incriminating statements ever. "You will never find my DNA on that broken paper clip. I was smart enough to wear gloves."

Final Analysis

The case was solved due to the investigator's ability to evaluate known case information:

1) Individuals who are widely loathed stand a much better chance of eventually being killed than most others.

2) The dead man was available to any one of several individuals who might have committed the crime.

3) The likelihood that the victim actually dropped the weights onto his own forehead was practically nonexistent.

4) Therefore, there was probably a crime, and it had to have taken place within the concept that nobody in the office had entered the office where the death took place.

5) At the outset of any given crime it may not be known what items present at the crime scene may have been connected to that crime.
6) Thus, the question became, how could the murder have been committed with what was known about the case and with what was physically present at the crime scene.
7) The manner in which the crime took place became apparent once all other considerations about the crime were ignored.
8) It had to have happened as it did.

# CASE 11

## READING AND UNDERSTANDING CASE FACTS

Investigative Overview

Criminal investigators are rightly products of their own professional experiences. Murder victims found in their own houses are often victims of domestic battery. Victims killed in a hotel are often killed by a hotel guest or employee; and persons killed in their workplace are often murdered as a direct result of their employment.

Certainly it is fine for an investigator to look at the relative probability that a new case might be more of the same; predictable motives for murder. However, one primary key to investigative success is the ability to weigh known facts of the case as a means of determining likely motives.

In the following case there were any number of known features, which argued strongly against the theory that the victim had been killed in the course of a bungled robbery. As you will read, the investigators were never influenced away from the theory that the motive had been robbery.

# CASE 11

The Crime

Joan Urbana, a young woman employed as the manager of a hamburger chain, was shot and killed behind a counter in the restaurant in the early morning hours. The following facts of the case were provided by a worker who survived the crime:

1) The victim and employee stayed more than two hours past the normal closing time to prepare for a corporate inspection scheduled for the following morning.

2) As the pair were leaving the restaurant, they were approached by two men – one short and light complected, the other tall and dark. The smaller of the two displayed a handgun and said, "You know what I want."

3) The victim then reopened the restaurant and everyone went inside.

4) The male worker was instructed to go into the men's washroom and stay there.

5) Moments later the worker heard a single gunshot immediately followed by a scream.

6) Soon after the police arrived having responded to a burglar alarm.

7) Police found the employee in the washroom and found the victim dead behind the service counter.

Police learned that money in the safe was not accessible due to having been on a time lock. A small amount of cash was left behind in the cash register. Investigators decided that the apparent motive was robbery and proceeded along those lines in working their case.

Observation of the restaurant disclosed several other pieces of information, which enter into the process of attempting to arrive at certain case determinations.

1) The building is situated across the width of the property with a customer parking lot in the front.

2) The parking lot of an office complex across the road offers the same view of the restaurant as does the restaurant lot.

3) The view inside is of the dining area only from either observation point. The area where orders are taken is to the right of the dining room and cannot be seen from the front of the business.

4) The kitchen is to the rear of the service counter and once again cannot be seen from the parking lot.

5) The public washrooms are just inside the front entrance to the restaurant to the right as one enters. The doors are kept locked and require being buzzed in by an employee. There is an inside lock to the washrooms.

6) Entrance into the counter and kitchen area requires use of a key pad and is made from a door on the side opposite the restrooms.

7) A view from the side of the dining room and into the counter area is possible from a window facing the building's side. Beyond that

window is an exit onto the ramp of a highway and has no parking spaces.

## Assessment of Case Facts

This case was treated by the police as a robbery gone wrong and after several years the crime remained unsolved. At that point a close friend of the victim visited a cold case investigator and asked that he review the case, hopefully to locate new leads. The cold case investigator then began looking at possible solutions.

## The Usual and the Unusual

One of the first considerations surrounding any crime is whether the act took place in a routine manner, meaning whether all aspects of the offense might have been expected. For example, in this case the gunmen surfaced at a time hours later than the victim and surviving employee would normally have gone home.

This condition therefore raises the question as to whether the gunmen waited for the workers to complete their tasks or simply happened along at the time they were leaving the restaurant. If the gunmen did wait long after the employees should have gone home, just where did they wait? Two men standing in front of a closed business in the middle of the night certainly might cause police interest as would sitting in an auto in an otherwise empty parking lot. They might have also parked across the road in the office building's parking lot, which was somewhat more concealed from the road than was the restaurant.

However, there is one major problem with this consideration. Whether on foot or in an auto, the gunmen were inviting being stopped and questioned by police; and had that occurred, the gunman's weapon would have been discovered. In that instance it makes sense that the killers arrived only shortly before they expected the victim to be leaving the restaurant.

If the gunmen did not wait for the workers to leave the restaurant, then they just happened along at the time the employees were heading home and decided to confront them. The relative probability of that having taken place must be measured by certain observations; namely, that if the workers were cleaning in either the counter or kitchen areas, they could not have been seen either from the road or the parking lot as that view only allows a look at the dining room. The gunmen would have had to have occasion to look into the side window alongside the highway ramp to see the workers in the kitchen area.

Based on the above facts it seems most reasonable that the gunmen were waiting for the employees to leave the restaurant. The question then becomes one of motive. Police investigators remain of the opinion that the crime was an armed robbery attempt gone wrong. Speculation logically continues with the question of what was usual and what was not usual at the time of the murder.

On any other night the manager would have likely been leaving her job at least two hours earlier than she did on the night of her death. By applying the concept that it is probable that the gunmen did wait for them to leave work, a great question surfaces.

In what way did the late hour make the proposed armed robbery more desirable than to have committed the crime the night before or the night after?

As it happened, the strength of the robbery plan was flawed by the safe being time locked and therefore unavailable. The money drop would have taken place hours earlier before the cleaning project began if the victim followed routine policy. The question then becomes one of whether we should simply take the position that the gunmen were unaware that the funds in the safe would not be available or perhaps that the crime was totally spontaneous in nature and without any premeditation whatsoever.

Under what circumstances, then, might a situation evolve by which the shooter having killed the victim is understandable? Whether the gunmen waited for the workers to leave the restaurant or just happened upon them, they decided on forcing them back inside. Once inside, they placed the worker in the men's washroom, then walked the manager around the other side and behind the counter. Soon after she explained that she had no access to the safe. The gunmen either became angry or perhaps panicked and shot and killed the young woman.

Though it might have happened in that manner there are known aspects of the case that seemingly act against that theory. To begin with, murder is a big step in the sense that it greatly increases police attention above that routinely given to a simple armed robbery offense. Of far greater importance is the issue of whether it is reasonable that the killers would have at once had a reason great enough to kill the manager and at the same time decided not to also kill the employee whom they had placed in the washroom before the shooting.

While it is often risky business attempting to think along with killer, it is possible to make note of the fact that to kill one and not the other in this case is most inconsistent in nature. Whether driven by either anger or panic, it is not reasonable that the dynamics that led to the shooting were not sustained long enough to also take the life of a prospective courtroom witness. Human emotions strong enough to cause what was done to the young woman seldom instantly evaporate into thin air.

## Making Determinations as to Motive

In order to believe that the victim was killed in a robbery attempt, one must also believe that the gunmen did embark on that project despite the following facts:

1) There was no money to be had.
2) The restaurant workers were present when they should have been long gone.
3) They killed the victim needlessly in that they allowed a witness to the crime to live.

## Facts Weighing Against a Robbery

If the crime was premeditated, it is then reasonable to assume that the gunmen knew that a clean-up project was underway, which would result in the workers leaving the restaurant far later than usual. However, anyone who might have had access to that information also should have known that the safe would be time-set. Once again the issue of consistency comes into play. Just as criminal behavior would generally dictate that neither or both of the victims be killed, it is also reasonable to accept the proposition that the gunmen would have known either or both facts of the case – that the workers would be there late and that the safe was locked, or neither of them.

Within this context it will be assumed that the surviving witness is being truthful as to events. Analysis of his account of facts does nothing whatsoever to support the robbery theory. He first states that the small light-skinned man produced a handgun and stated, "You know what I want." Police took that statement to mean that they wanted money, however that was never said.

Is it not possible that the gunman's statement meant something entirely different to the murder victim? Certainly the gunman's words were not clearly indicative of robbery as a motive.

The worker also stated that he was placed in a washroom before his manager was shot and killed. Once again accepting that as true, at least for now, what advantage might the gunmen have enjoyed by separating the pair prior to committing an armed robbery? One thing is certain – there is very little of a secretive nature attached to the statement, "Give me your money." There is no apparent reason to deliver such a message privately. By contrast, if the gunmen had some other reason for approaching the young woman at gunpoint, they might have had the best of all reasons to wish to speak to her privately.

The most important question to be asked of the surviving worker is whether it seemed to him that the gunmen and victim seemed to have known one another. If they did know each other, then it is certain that she did know what it was that they actually wanted.

What Then, if Not a Robbery?

Based on the premise that most murder victims are killed by people they know, investigators conduct thorough background checks of the victim. This fact often results in the surfacing of a motive for wanting a victim dead. The new suspect is then evaluated within the context of all other known facts of the case in order to determine whether that party fits the framework of the crime. In many such instances the case against the suspect quickly comes together.

In this instance it is possible that some person close to the victim might have wanted her dead to the extent that they themselves may have been involved in the carrying out of the crime. Or perhaps they might have arranged for the crime. It is important to note that none of this has apparently been attended to by the police investigators based on their assuredness that the victim was killed by would-be robbers.

One might have gathered a list of men close to the victim and gained photos of each so that the surviving employee might view a photo gallery of suspects. This simple step would be a quick and uncomplicated means of eliminating the idea that the murder was carried out directly by such a person. It does not matter in the least whether it is thought that it is unlikely, possible, or probable that it happened that way, it just needs to be done. Within the inner circles of criminal investigation such routine activities to eliminate all possibilities is called "covering the bases."

In the event that someone close to the victim was responsible for the crime, the probability is great that they would have been more likely to arrange for the crime than to have actually carried it out themselves. This is true for the obvious reason that they would be aware the police might investigate as described above.

Motives for murder range from simple to those deeply buried and complex. As an employee of a national chain of restaurants, it is likely that the victim had some type of life insurance policy. Within the broadest of terms a beneficiary of such a policy becomes a potential suspect. Should investigation disclose that the victim's relationship with the beneficiary was in deteriorating stages, then a full-blown motive comes to the surface. Many cases are solved in just such a simple manner.

## Making Sense of Conditions

One of the most intriguing aspects of the Urbana case was the statement made by the gunman to the victim outside the restaurant, "You know what I want." The witness said that the victim responded with something of an ironic smile. One explanation for the killer's words and the victim's response might be that she knew exactly what the incident was about, the implication being that she knew it was something somehow different than a robbery. She might have either personally known the gunmen or perhaps simply knew who they were.

## A Theory Conforming to Case Facts

The victim and her husband Jeffrey had met several years earlier in an alcohol and drug treatment program. The victim had since remained clean and sober until the time of her death. It was thought at the time that Jeffrey also continued practicing recovery. The recovery issue might be important in the sense that both the victim and her husband had past lives that included members of the criminal community. Perhaps the gunmen were people from the victim's life prior to getting clean and sober. Or they might have been individuals she knew from her recovery life who did not stay clean and thus reverted to their criminal ways.

In either case such individuals might have decided that Joan Urbana would practice loyalty to old friends and would allow the robbery to occur and would not report to the police that she knew the gunmen. This theory is strong in the sense that this would account for why the offenders separated the helper by placing him in the washroom, so that they could get her assurance that she would keep their secret. Based on the theory as stated, the victim would have been likely to have told them that she was going to tell the police what had happened and who they were. Thus the shooting only seconds after his having been placed in the washroom. A variation of the same theory is that Jeffrey Urbana was no longer clean and sober, and he set up the crime making use of old friends known to the victim. Another possibility is that the victim knew the offenders and thought at the outset that the gunmen who she knew were there to commit a robbery, but actually they had been hired to execute her in the workplace in the hope that the police would do exactly what they did and take the crime as a bungled robbery.

The Aftermath

Jeffrey Urbana seemingly had two strong motives for wishing the victim dead. First, he received a great deal of money through the victim's corporate life insurance policy. Second, immediately after her death he renewed old acquaintances with a woman who he and Joan had met in treatment. The victim's family was uniformly convinced that Jeffrey was behind the victim's death. They passed along a copy of the victim's diary where she wrote on several occasions that she was convinced that Jeffrey had carried on with this other woman throughout the course of their marriage.

251

Investigators are uniformly taught early on that coincidences are never to be believed until such time as they can be proven to exist. Based on that concept, consider the following:

1) Family and friends gathered the night before Joan's funeral. Joan's mother Maggie was there with her sister and a dozen other women.

2) Jeffrey sat in the corner holding hands with a woman. When asked who she was, he said it was his sister. They knew it was not a sister.

3) The next morning Joan's mother was preparing to attend her child's funeral when she died in the bathtub in Joan and Jeffrey's apartment.

4) Jeffrey notified the police that his mother-in-law died of a heart attack stemming from the stress of her daughter's death.

5) Police did not send Maggie's remains to the medical examiner's office to establish a cause of death.

6) Cold case investigators verified that Jeffrey and his old friend from drug treatment lived together within a week of the two deaths and remained together for at least several years thereafter.

Cold Case Investigative Steps

1) There is a police composite sketch of the shooter in the case. There is also a physical description of his much taller accomplice who

wore a black shirt with a yellow letter "G" on it at the time of the crime.

2) The murder of Joan Urbana took place in the suburb not far from a major city.

3) The victim's house where her mother died in the bathtub was located in that city.

4) The husband Jeffrey grew up in that same neighborhood where they lived at the time of the deaths.

5) The woman he took up with immediately after the murder also lived in the same city.

6) It was learned that Jeffrey had resumed his drug use in the years after the murder or murders.

7) Since the new woman had been in rehab with the victim and Jeffrey, it is safe to assume that she probably also practiced recovery life but for how long is unknown.

Investigative Issues

While the police were showing the composite sketch of the shooter in the suburbs while searching for armed robbers, if the murder of Joan Urbana was connected in any way to her husband, then the killers would be far more likely to have been associates of his from the city. Tactical and narcotics officers might recognize the composite sketch as looking like an individual they know.

The black and yellow shirt worn by the second offender may have been a tribute to street gang colors. In the era of the crime, colors of athletic apparel were commonly worn in conjunction with gang affiliation. Perhaps the shirt was from

Grambling State University whose colors are black and yellow.

Three pieces of information about the husband's new girlfriend: The victim was convinced that he was seeing her during the time leading up to her death; she was with him immediately after the murder; and she seemingly was with him at whatever time he began once again using drugs. Taken together, it is hard to imagine any circumstance whereby she did not know that he was in some way involved in his wife's death. Thus, the question becomes under what conditions might she tell what she knows to investigators. Seemingly, the notion of the girl friend talking is best linked to whether or not she remains clean and in drug recovery.

Much of the teachings of the 12-Step recovery model deal with two issues. The first is that whatever one places ahead of their recovery is the first thing they will use upon relapse. The second is that the fastest road to relapse is to be involved with others who are using drugs or alcohol. Therefore, if Jeffrey Urbana's girlfriend is most serious about staying clean and sober, she may have broken up with the subject. Under such conditions she would be relatively likely to be honest with authorities and tell what she knows. There is also the recurring issue that less involved offenders often are given an opportunity to turn state's evidence and become a witness against the more involved party.

## The Bathtub Death

Family members stand together in their collective belief that Jeffrey Urbana first had Joan killed and then physically killed his mother-in-law in response to her having accused him of being responsible for the first crime. Had he already set upon Joan's death he stood to lose her insurance settlement if Maggie began accusing him publicly of the crime. Thus, he would have had little to lose in committing the bathtub crime as well.

## Investigative Uniqueness

This case is interesting in the sense that the possibility exists that the same offender killed two different people over a five-day period. Yet the manner in which the two incidents might be brought to case solution are totally different. In the restaurant murder of Joan Urbana investigators must either identify the killers through their descriptions, then get them to tell who if anyone hired them, or they must get the girlfriend to tell what she knows about Jeffrey Urbana's involvement in his wife's death.

By contrast there are clearly no third parties capable of stating just what went on between Jeffrey Urbana and his mother-in-law, Maggie, as they prepared to attend Joan's funeral. Rather, this case hinges totally on forensic evidence. If Joan's mother were murdered, a pathologist would be able to learn that by exhuming the body and searching for evidence of drowning in the bathtub, strangulation, or blunt trauma injuries. If any of these were present, Jeffrey Urbana would have a serious problem on his hands, since he was alone in the apartment with his deceased mother-in-law when he called 911 to report her death in the bathtub.

## Order of Events

Keep in mind that the two deaths occurred in different jurisdictions, thus two investigative bodies would be involved in taking whatever actions required. If the Joan Urbana investigation indicated or proved Jeffrey's involvement, then the other jurisdiction would surely consider that he might have killed his mother-in-law as well. Under those conditions they would then take it upon themselves to exhume her remains in order to search for foul play. However, without progress on the first crime it is doubtful that they would see fit to perform an autopsy.

However, the family has the right to order that an individual be exhumed. Without the support of the authorities the family would then have to retain a private medical examiner to search for cause of death. Such a doctor would have to be noted in the field so that if his findings indicated that the individual was murdered, such an opinion would be accepted as valid.

Suppose that the family did order a private autopsy of the mother-in-law and the findings did indicate foul play, then the theory that Jeffrey Urbana was responsible for both deaths would seem all but a certainty.

# CASE 12

## FAULTY RELIANCE ON EXTERNAL INVESTIGATIVE SOURCES

Investigative Overview

In many cases criminal investigations wear on for lengthy periods of time without as much as a single viable suspect having surfaced. By contrast, in this case a logical suspect surfaced early on. It was known that the suspect had unsuccessfully attempted to date the victim. Not only had he been rebuffed, but the victim was quite unkind in turning the suspect down. Moreover, the suspect was convicted of attempting to choke another young woman to death. Just as importantly, there was a circumstantial witness to the murder who provided the police with a composite sketch of a suspect. The sketch looked as if the suspect had modeled for it.

The police then picked up the suspect and had him take a polygraph test. The suspect passed the lie detector to the satisfaction of the police, and thereafter was disregarded as a suspect despite the overwhelming evidence of guilt. It mattered little that researchers of polygraph testing have consistently determined that the lie detector process can be easily defeated by simple steps taken by suspects, and generally is no more reliable than a simple flip of the coin.

# CASE 12

## The Crime

Kori Kraft was a coed at a medium-sized university. On a cold winter night the victim and her girlfriend left their respective part-time jobs, stopped for a beer, and then walked back toward campus. They lived a block or two from one another and walked until they arrived at a fork in the road. Kori turned right toward her sorority house, and Juanita King headed off to the apartment she shared with two friends. It was about 9 p.m. by the time Kori arrived at her building.

The next morning at about 10:30 a.m. students found Kori Kraft unconscious alongside the sorority house. She had suffered a massive head injury and was transported to a local hospital. It was quickly determined that she had hypothermia from apparently having been outside in the cold all night after having been attacked not long after having arrived home the night before. Once the severity of her head injuries was determined, she was air-transported to a larger hospital. After five hours of treatment Kori Kraft died of her blunt trauma injuries.

Police recovered a length of a railroad tie near the crime scene but never stated whether or not they found blood or hair evidence matching the victim's wounds. Two years after the crime the case remained unsolved. It was alleged that one of the police investigators gave the railroad tie to a criminal justice professor at the university, who used the probable weapon as a conversation piece in his faculty office.

Early Investigation

A witness came forward and told the police that she had seen a female on her knees in a doubled-over position with two men standing over her. The larger of the two was a big burly fellow with a full beard, who had a large length of wood in this hand. The second man had light hair. A composite sketch of the bearded suspect was created.

Many of the victim's friends told police about a student who resembled the composite sketch that they suspected for the following reasons in addition to his physical appearance:

1) He seemed obsessed with the victim.
2) He frequented a restaurant/bar that the victim frequented.
3) He had asked Kori out; she not only refused his offer but mocked the suspect in the process.
4) The suspect was known for his rageful behavior.
5) He was a known street drug user.

Certain other incriminating facts linking the suspect to the crime will be outlined in the "Cold Case" section of this piece.

———————

After the first year or so it appeared as if very little was done by the police. No wonder then that the Kori Kraft case would eventually become the oldest unsolved murder in that state's listings of old crimes.

––––––––––––––––

A cold case investigator with a reasonably successful track record began looking at the case some thirty years after the crime. Contact was made with the university library, which agreed to assist in gathering old newspaper clippings on the case, both from the local city and university newspapers. Inroads were made into the academic community and several past and present professors recalled certain aspects of the case.

Several such sources told essentially the same story: An officer of the university student senate had a rich history of out-of-control rage. Moreover, the suspect looked "just like" the composite sketch of the individual holding the piece of wood in his hand as observed by the witness. Names of various individuals connected with the university student senate were researched. Before long it was learned that the party mentioned with the violent temper had actually been the senate past president. His name was Arturo Brand.

Once the suspect's name had been established, it was possible to learn far more about him. A newspaper article reported that Brand had been charged with having physically attacked another coed a few months after Kori Kraft's death.

Had a search for that victim been conducted soon after the crime, her location would have almost certainly been a short process. However some thirty years later there was the matter of attempting to track a woman who, as it turned out, had changed her last name several times based on marriages and divorces. She was eventually located in a southern state; and when first contacted by phone, she once again became terrified at the thought of her encounter with Arturo Brand more than three decades earlier. She gave the following account of facts:

1) She had met Brand among a group of people and had simply said hello to him.

2) The next time she saw him he acted as if they were close friends, which gave her "chills."

3) The third time she saw him was outside a bar and he was "stoned" and "blind drunk."

4) He approached her and tried to put his arms around her.

5) She told him loudly to leave her alone, at which time he began punching her repeatedly in the face.

6) Once she was knocked to the ground, Brand jumped on top of her and began strangling her with his hands.

7) As she was losing consciousness, several people pulled Brand off of her and, in her opinion, saved her life.

8) Brand was arrested and charged only with misdemeanor battery.

9) Brand was found guilty a year later and sentenced to periodic confinement.

## Investigative Assessment

Arturo Brand was an ex-Marine who always wore combat boots. This was of interest since Kori Kraft had been the victim of a home invasion in her sorority house eighteen months before her death. In that case a large man wearing combat boots entered her bedroom as she slept. She was yanked out of bed, and the attacker placed his hand over her face and mouth. As she screamed for help, she was able to see that the attacker wore combat boots.

The cold case investigator learned that Arturo Brand had asked for a tour of the victim's sorority house in conjunction with his having been a member of the university student senate. This was granted, thus Brand would have been able to learn the layout of where his intended victim lived, this in preparation for the intended home invasion.

---

As to the matter of homicide, the cold case investigation had disclosed that the suspect was apparently obsessed with Kori Kraft; she had mocked his request for a date with her; he acted as if he somehow had a close relationship with another coed; and when she rebuked his advances, he beat her brutally, then attempted to strangle her to death.

Seldom does any given suspect fit the model of the wanted offender more perfectly than did Brand match up as the killer in this case.

However, the strongest evidence was yet to surface. Kori Kraft's sorority sisters explained the following to the cold case investigator:

1) The murder took place during a semester break, therefore most of the students had returned to their homes.

2) At about noon, or within one hour of Kori having been found gravely injured, Arturo Brand called one of her friends at her home hundreds of miles away and told her, "Your friend Kori was beaten almost to death."

3) Several of Kori's sorority sisters lived in the city where she was hospitalized and met the victim's parents at the hospital. They were notified of her death at about 5 p.m.

4) In less than one hour of her death, Arturo Brand was once again on the phone, this time informing the president of the sorority that Kori had died.

---

Thoughtful investigators typically assume that when suspects of a crime know pieces of information about events that they should not reasonably know, that becomes an extremely strong form of incrimination. There is simply no way in which any casual observer could have learned first that the victim had been gravely attacked and then later of her death, both within a matter of moments after each event. The only reasonable explanation is that Brand was nearby watching the events as they unfolded, something that only the killer would do.

At the same time that the cold case investigator was told of the strange phone calls, it was also learned that those involved had told the police the same things within moments of having received the phone calls. One of the women called by Brand was so fearful that he was Kori's killer and would be seeking her out next, that the police escorted her to and from her classes for weeks after the murder.

It is impossible to see any possible way that the police would agree to act as bodyguards against the possible actions of Arturo Brand without having considered him a serious suspect immediately after the crime. However, numerous of Brand's friends were contacted by the cold case investigator, and all stated that Brand kept talking about how he expected to be picked up and questioned by the police. But according to Brand that never happened.

The last piece of evidence against Brand rests in the fact that photos of the suspect taken during the era of the crime look like he posed for the composite sketch. Numerous sources stated that in the months after Kori Kraft's murder students on campus would regularly approach Brand stating that they just saw his picture in a bunch of store windows, making reference to composite sketches pasted all around campus.

Thus the question becomes how might all of this incriminating evidence linking Brand to the crime have been common knowledge among everyone in this college town and yet have seemingly been lost on the police?

This is a prime example of why certain cases become first cold, then finally stone cold frozen.

A Turn of Events

The cold case investigator turned his file over to the police. During the meeting when that took place, the police:

1) Explained that despite what some might consider overwhelming indications of his guilt, they had eliminated Arturo Brand as a suspect in the murder of Kori Kraft because he had PASSED A POLYGRAPH TEST.

2) They were not interested in the further help of the cold case investigator.

3) They decided to reopen their investigation into the case and were assigning two patrol officers without prior investigative experience to conduct their own cold case investigation.

———————

Nearly two years later the case remained unsolved. Occasionally, some individuals close to one side of the case or the other would contact the cold case investigator to discuss developments. Shortly after the police were given the cold case file, the sergeant in charge of investigations was sent unceremoniously back to the patrol division. There was much speculation that he lost his investigative job because he might have suggested to administrators that they should rely on the civilian cold case investigator who seemed to "have the case right." Police administrators and the local prosecutors were not about to allow a "city slicker" to show them up – after all, all investigators are pretty much equal.

It was also stated that the police investigators never did work the case in terms of Arturo Brand's involvement, based on their belief in the reliability of the polygraph testing process. That the police did nothing with regard to Brand was also verified by an old associate of his who ran into him in the state where he has lived for many years. When told that the Kraft case was being reinvestigated by the police, Brand is alleged to have commented that the city police could not find a black Buick in a bathtub, further stating that nobody had contacted him about the case for decades.

---

Review of Polygraph Literature

In one funded research project it was determined that the polygraph test is far more effective on property offenders than on violent offenders. The same research disclosed that the least effective police departments are most likely to trust and use the polygraph and that there are scores of tested methods of defeating the polygraph examination.

A University of Utah research stated that the test is easily defeated by biting one's tongue, stepping on a thumbtack placed inside one's shoe, counting backwards by sevens during questioning, and by taking a barbiturate drug that slows the central nervous system so that the machine cannot get a reading.

However, the problems with polygraph testing goes far deeper than simple efforts to defeat the process. The late Chicago Police homicide investigator, Thomas Flanagan, said it best to new investigators in pre-service training:

"So take a guy who puts a gun in his victim's face. The guy doesn't fight, does just what he was told to do, but when the robbery is over the robber smiles and shoots the guy in the face just for the fun of it. Who in their right mind would actually believe that psychopaths like that are going to get nervous because they're hooked up to a lie detector? Criminals like that can look anyone in the face and tell you whatever you want to hear. Talk to any killer and they'll tell you that death row is full of guys who laugh about having passed polygraph tests given by guys with their heads up their butt."

------------------

## Prologue

The civilian cold case investigator interested a federal law enforcement agency in following up on the Kori Kraft case and Arturo Brand as the killer. Their jurisdiction is established by a law, which states that when an offender leaves the state of the crime's occurrence in order to avoid investigation and prosecution, the federal government may assume investigative authority. Agents are optimistic at arriving at case solution based on what they termed as "an overwhelming number of indicators of (his) guilt."

# CASE 13

# THE INTERROGATION FEATURE
# OF CRIMINAL INVESTIGATION

## Investigative Overview

Bright criminal investigators interrogate by confronting an apparently guilty suspect with known facts of the case, which tend to link that suspect to the crime. To the extent that the suspect sees the strong probability that he/she will be (1) criminally charged, and (2) convicted of the crime, he is likely to do whatever he sees as possible to lighten his perilous condition.

Criminal suspects commonly know that confessions to the police typically lead to plea bargaining, and that plea bargaining leads to reduced sentences. Thus, at the moment that a guilty suspect feels that he has no other way out, his is likely to privately consider the benefits of confessing to the crime, implicating accomplices, and otherwise cooperating with the investigative cause.

# CASE 13

*Author's Note: Case 13 is presented in three parts, each dealing with similar issues connected to the custodial interrogation issue. They are designated as Parts A, B, and C. Each individual part will include an analysis, then at the end there will be a general conclusion presented.*

*PART A:*

Three men were riding around a high-crime-rate urban area. The driver of the car ended up shot in the head. The driver's side window was shattered, supporting the survivors' contention that a gunman on the street shot and killed their friend.

The alleged witnesses did behave suspiciously in the aftermath of the shooting. Their explanations for having been in the area changed from seeking cheap gas for the car, to buying marijuana, to looking to buy cocaine. As the pair waited for the police to respond to the crime, they were seen arguing with one another, indicating that they were perhaps getting their story together in advance of speaking to the police.

The angle of the gunshot wound to the victim's head indicated it came more from the rear than from the left and through the shattered window. All in all, there were reasons to question the identity of the actual shooter.

One thing the two survivors of the shooting did agree on was that one of them was riding on the front passenger seat, the other in the rear.

### Where to Start

While the fatal bullet may or may not have entered the car from the outside, what is certain is that the bullet could not have been fired from the position of the passenger in the front seat. Thus, the victim was either shot by a stranger on the street or by the passenger sitting to the rear of the victim.

At the outset of any murder investigation an essential task is to attempt to determine motive based on known case facts. In this instance three young men were driving about in a community where the featured products are drugs, sex for hire, and the inevitable resulting violence. It is also to be noted that there was beer and marijuana in the car, and the victim's toxicology findings were that he had used marijuana and was intoxicated. Thus, it is also reasonable to assume that the survivor-suspects were also high at the time of the crime.

Those under the influence lose their inhibitions, therefore attempting to assign reason and logic to such crimes can be a mistake. Where alcohol and drugs are involved it could have been an accidental shooting, or it might have been an argument over who gets first hit from a joint.

One possible theory is that the trio was cruising the inner-city in order to make some quick money, perhaps by sticking up a drug dealer. Taken one step beyond, it is possible that the driver owed money to the passenger in the back, and the driver was looking to make fast illegal money to pay him off. This possibility would account for their driving around while the passenger in the back held the driver at gunpoint.

---

## The Interrogation

What is clearly known is that if the victim were not killed from a shot outside the car, he was killed by a shot from the back seat. Since Suspect 1 willingly placed himself alone in the back, and Suspect 2 admitted to having been alongside the victim, what is clear is that both suspects do know what actually took place.

The usual application of the law is that if two or more offenders enter into a crime that results in murder, all parties are legally accountable despite not having actually pulled the trigger that took the life. However, both offenders do not feel the same responsibility; therefore, it is always wise for the police interrogator to begin by talking to the less active and accountable suspect.

In this case the police may wish to begin by talking to Suspect 2, telling him that the main concern of the authorities is to prove a case against the actual shooter, allowing the suspect from the front seat an opportunity to claim either surprise at the shooting or the contention that he was powerless to stop the attack by the shooter.

When accomplices do provide the police with such information, it is usual that they will follow up with what they told the police by testifying against the shooter at trial. In such instances prosecutors typically allow the less involved suspect to enter a plea of guilty in return for a reduced sentence.

It is to be noted that the added advantage to the authorities is that this case might never have been solved with the less involved suspect's admission of guilt.

Case Solution

The interrogator explained to Suspect 2 that the angle of the gunshot wound clearly determined that the fatal bullet could not have been fired through the auto window. That left only one other choice – the victim was killed by a gunshot fired from the back seat of the car. As such, either Suspect 1 or Suspect 2 was the shooter. Whichever suspect did not fire the shot was indeed an eyewitness and an accomplice at that.

Faced with the unpleasant proposition of going to prison for life for the work of another, Suspect 2 told the story. The three of them had been driving around drinking beer and smoking marijuana while the driver looked for a dealer to rip off. It seems that the driver did owe Suspect 1 a large amount of money from a previous drug deal gone wrong, and the driver needed to make it right. While all of this was going on, the weapon in Suspect 1's hand discharged in the back seat, striking the victim in the head. Suspect 1 would later say that the gun simply went off and the shooting was accidental. Criminal charges are pending.

PART B:

A young woman's naked remains were found in a landfill area. She had been badly beaten about the face and head, and a large screw had been impacted into her neck. Police investigation disclosed the following:

1) She had stopped at her estranged boyfriend's home at about 2 a.m. She walked off after a short conversation with him.

2) A friend of the boyfriend was observed beating the victim with his fists on a nearby main street at about 3 a.m. The witness told the attacker to stop.

3) The witness did not see anyone with the attacker.

4) The attacker told police that he and a friend had been driving around the area of the attack during the time in question.

5) Two other friends likewise placed themselves driving in the area in a second car.

6) At 5 a.m. the neighbors heard moans coming from an alley two blocks from where the witness had seen the beating take place. Blood and a wig the victim had been wearing were in the alley.

---

Observations

Based on the witness observations and the suspect's own statement it seems likely that the other three associates of the attacker collaborated in placing the victim's injured body in the nearby alley. Later, it is possible that the attacker or the attacker and friends may have decided that the victim's positioning in the alley was too close to where the witness saw the beating occur. If so, all concerned may well have moved the victim to the landfill location farther away.

It is likely that the attacker, with or without his companions, stripped the victim naked in an attempt to make it appear that her attack was sexually motivated. At the same time somebody drove the large screw into the victim's neck. This wound may have been the immediate cause of death; however, it is also possible that the victim would have soon died as a result of the initial beating to her head and face.

The Interrogation

Three possible accomplices placed themselves driving around in the immediate area of the beating on the street. One such accomplice was likely present nearby at the time of the beating though the witness did not see him there. Two others placed themselves in a second car driving about nearby.

The relative involvement of each possible accomplice is based on whether or not they were present when the apparent fatal wound was inflicted with the screw driven into the victim's neck. Perhaps one or more of them actually participated in inflicting what proved to be the fatal wound. If all were present, all are equally accountable. Thus there may be no advantage to interrogating one before the others.

Special Considerations

There are times when the secrets of co-conspirators are flimsy at best. This is especially true on old and cold cases. When a crime is new, the offenders spend much time considering whether or not they will get away with the crime. However, with the passing of time without police contacting them, suspects become more and more confident in their ability to beat the case. Then suddenly after years or even decades there is a police investigation anew.

Once one offender learns of the cold case investigation great efforts are often made to notify the others involved. A simple police check of the suspects' phone records often reaffirms their complicity in the offense.

Bright investigators then take advantage of this new alarm by quickly interrogating whichever suspect they think to be the most vulnerable among the group. The interrogation tactic is to simply state that the first suspect to cooperate gets the best deal with authorities. In this manner the interrogator is stating that he is certain that at least one suspect will cave in and talk. Thus, guilty suspects may feel extreme pressure to be the first to talk.

---

In Part B it is known that the first suspect did beat the victim with his fists before a witness. It is then surmised that at least one and possibly three accomplices helped move the victim once and possibly twice. It also seems likely that some of the same group had to have been present when the large screw was driven into the victim's neck.

Though each party would then be legally accountable for the victim's death, it remains possible that the state would allow the most willing of the crew to testify against the others in return for sentencing consideration.

PART C

Investigative Summary

A newspaper delivery driver and his helper were robbed at gunpoint for the second time within one week by the same offender. In the first instance neither the driver nor his helper were injured. However, on the second occasion the robber placed a handgun to the victim's stomach and fired twice. As the criminal investigation began, the driver was fighting for his life.

Early Investigation

Well-trained investigators act against the existence of coincidences. In this case it was duly noted that the pair of newspaper employees had been robbed twice by the same offender within several blocks of one another. Thus the question became what possible reason did the same offender have to stick up the same workers within such a short period of time.

The investigators were able to speak to the gravely injured victim in the hospital, asking whether he thought it likely that the helper had orchestrated the two robberies with the shooter. The victim said that he and the helper were close friends and that the helper had been a guest for dinner in his home in the past.

The investigators then interviewed the helper who also described the gunman for the purpose of creating a composite sketch. Despite the kind words by the victim about the helper, the investigators continued to consider that he had set up the crime.

The Interrogation

The interrogators told the helper the truth about various aspects of the case. Since the victims worked for a major city newspaper, the case was going to remain on the front page of the paper until the case was solved. The helper was also truthfully told that the case was a "heater" in that the mayor was calling the police chief every few hours to inquire about case progress. In short, the interrogators mapped out the fact that this investigation was not going anywhere until the shooter was charged.

The interrogators shifted gears, explaining to the helper that the state was primarily interested in charging the gunman who actually pulled the trigger. In the interest of proving the case against the shooter they would gladly work with others who were less involved.

While all of this was being said to the helper, he became more and more unsettled. He fidgeted with a paper clip on the table and began poking the unfolded metal edge against the palm of his hand. Before long, the hand was bleeding. The helper was nervous.

The interrogators asked the helper if he thought that they would find the truth. The helper nodded, stating that he knew that they knew their business. They then told the helper that now was the time to come clean because if they learned on their own that the helper was involved, there would be no breaks given later on.

## The Admission

Within an hour's time the helper explained that the shooter was his half-brother, who had just been released from prison for attempted murder. The shooter intimidated him into telling him where and when the delivery truck would be along. At the date and time in question the gunman jumped onto the truck for the second time within a week and robbed and shot the victim for good measure.

In this case the helper was charged with conspiracy to commit armed robbery. After his having testified at trial against his half-brother, he received a greatly reduced prison sentence. Fortunately, the shooting victim did survive his wounds and was present when the shooter was sentenced to seventy-five years in prison.

## Final Observation

This is a prime example of a case unlikely to have been solved had it not been for the cooperation of a lesser-involved offender. The prosecutor was eager enough to solve this high profile case that extending the best plea-bargaining deal possible to the helper was an easy decision.

# CASE 14

# A COMPARATIVE ANALYSIS OF
# TWO MASS MURDERS

<u>Making Sense of Known Case Facts</u>
Homicide cases are routinely solved by bright investigators who recognize certain facts of a case before creating an investigative theory that accounts for how the crime was carried out. One such investigative theory might deal with establishing a motive for the crime. Was the offense committed by a stranger or by someone with whom they knew in life? Making this initial determination is of key importance if for no other reason than the places one searches for strangers is totally separate from sifting through a list of persons of the victim's relationships in search of someone with a motive for the crime.

<u>Categories of Killers</u>
Differing groups of killers typically go about their respective crimes in significantly different ways. Most random killers wish to act quickly based on the concept that the sooner one successfully flees the crime scene, the greater their chances are of escaping detection and apprehension. By way of contrast, many serial killers must accomplish certain tasks in the course of their crimes, many of which are time-consuming. Victims of serial offenders are often subjected to overkill, that is, multiple causes of death or mutilation. Wise investigators, therefore, weigh

time-consuming killings as likely being the work of a serial offender.

## Intelligence of Killers

Police investigators often engage in their development while operating on the concept that, "if the killer was smart they would have behaved in a certain way." Operating on such a perspective often leads to quick case solution, but only when the offender planned the crime based on that which is logical. However, the opposite is also often true – many of the most difficult cases to solve are those where the crime itself or the manner in which it was carried out is simply illogical. One simple way to summarize such situations is that criminal investigators may get lost while seeking logic where the behaviors and method of operation were both illogical and perhaps downright unintelligent on the part of the killer. Simply put, investigators can give suspects more credit than they are due.

## Grasping for Motives

In one unsolved murder, a young woman was shot point-blank in the restaurant where she worked. Investigators quickly decided that she was killed in the course of a bungled robbery attempt. One might therefore assume that the investigation centered on considering known robbers as suspects. Objective analysis of known case facts strongly disputes the robbery theory. Consider: (1) the daily proceeds had long since been placed in a drop safe, therefore no funds were available to the offenders; (2) the crime took place three hours after the restaurant closed for the evening and they were present at the time of the crime only because they stayed after to clean the store; and (3) the display lighting was off and stalking would-be robbers could not have seen inside the store to know the victim was present. All of these case features argue that the crime was not robbery-related. Unfortunately, it is common investigative error to assume that when a victim is killed at a workplace that the motive must be work-related. Consider the husband who wishes his wife dead; to have her killing occur at work hopefully implies to the police that the crime was connected to her work and not based on the husband's actual motive for the crime.

Brown's Chicken Massacre Overview

On January 8, 1993, seven persons were killed inside the restaurant in Palatine, Illinois. Richard Ehlenfeldt and his wife, Lynn, were the owners killed, along with five other employees. All were shot to death except for Lynn Ehlenfeldt who was stabbed multiple times. The killers apparently entered the restaurant just before its 9 p.m. closing. The victims were then forced into the back room of the store where they were executed.

Police Investigation

For much of the investigation, the police treated the crime as a robbery. However, a review of files did not result in statements indicating that funds were actually taken in the course of the incident. To the extent that investigators believed that the primary motive for the crime was actually robbery, they would likely be searching for known robbers and other potential strangers to the victims as suspects.

## Weighing the Robbery Theory

All criminal investigations need to be viewed and analyzed from the perspective of the offender(s). Within that context, it is safe to assert that the execution of multiple victims is a lot for the killers to take on. Had the offender simply walked into the store and pulled a gun demanding money, the responding police might have spent anywhere from a few hours to a few days searching for a case solution. By contrast, a mass murder investigation can be depended on to last literally years and even decades.

In fictional crime productions, victims are killed to prevent them from later identifying the offenders. However, in real life, the taking of a life simply causes too much "heat." One simple option to killing potential witnesses would simply be to wear a ski mask to the crime. Given that this offense took place in winter season, such ski masks would not have attracted attention or concern.

## Making Sense of Known Case Facts

Investigators are able to arrive at motives based on the killer's method of operation. To the extent that crime analysis states that the killing of seven persons is too great a risk to pay for whatever money was present in the store, then robbery was probably not the actual primary motive. Bright and experienced investigators learn that determining unusual aspects of a crime often lead to the surfacing of a motive.

In this case, six victims were shot execution style while Lynn Ehlenfeldt was repeatedly stabbed. This observation is telling in two different ways. First, a second cause of death in and of itself is a difference. That variance from the shooting of the others was more likely intended as opposed to having been a mere coincidence. Second, repeatedly stabbing one victim among the others seemingly singles them out as different in the eyes of the killer(s).

Killer Profile

It is important to note that switching from quickly executing victims with a firearm to the much more time-consuming stabbing of one select victim not only indicates that the victim being killed in a different manner than the others means something different to the attacker. Additionally, taking extra time at the crime scene clearly indicates the importance of taking that one life precisely as carried out.

When such variances within the course of carrying out a crime occurs, the nature of the variance should be taken by investigators as a strong indicator that the victim treated and killed differently was the actual target. In that sense, the other victims of the mass murder may well have simply been slain by the killer in order to attempt to obscure the identity and motive of killing only one targeted victim.

Consider the Brown's Case as to possible motives for the crime. Choice I is that the motive was robbery. Investigators might then investigate literally hundreds of known robbers as possible killers. Choice II might be as simple as the investigative theory that the killers simply went on a senseless errand of death indiscriminately killing innocent victims. In either such case, the investigators might have spent weeks, months or even years looking into either or both of the above investigative theories, when all along the actual motive for the mass slayings was to accomplish the death of a single target. As such, all of the others may have been killed for the specific reason of obscuring the fact the killer had a motive for the killing of only one victim.

Thus the Theory

Based on the above theory development, one might argue that it was reasonable and logical to investigate along the lines that the killer was someone who wished to kill the co-owner of the store, Lynn Ehlenfeldt, and that all of the others were killed either because they happened to be present at the time or they were killed to obscure the motive for killing the intended victim. Since the crime took place in the store, one might have considered that the killer(s) actually knew the victim from her work there.

Actual Case Outcome

Since this case was actually solved a decade after the event, we do know its outcome, thus one might argue that the case theory presented here is tainted by actual knowledge of the debriefing of the suspects.

Two teenagers, Juan Luna and Jim Degorski, were charged and convicted of the mass murder. The case was cracked when a former girlfriend of Degorski came forward and told the following account of events. The two offenders entered the store and ordered food. They then drew weapons and forced their intended victims into the back room where the executions of six victims by gunshot wounds took place. The female owner, Lynn Ehlenfeldt, was stabbed multiple times by Luna. The offenders then went to the informant's apartment and played music and bragged of having committed the crime as stated above.

It is to be noted that Juan Luna was a former employee of the Brown's Chicken in question. An analysis of the case facts follow.

1) Luna and his accomplice, Degorski, entered the store in the knowledge that at least certain persons working there at that time would recognize him and known his name.

2) Thus, the possibility of the pair successfully robbing the store was virtually nonexistent.

3) Therefore, the primary motive for the crime would not have been robbery.

4) Based on Luna's willingness to pull a handgun on intended victims, the offenders' actual plan must have been to kill all persons present. To do anything else clearly would have led to Luna, who was known to the owners, if not other employees present, to be quickly named as the robber/gunman.

5) Thus, the logical conclusion is that the mass murder was clearly premeditated, for nothing short of that act might have prevented Juan Luna's arrest.
6) The differing cause of death upon the female owner is likely a telltale indication of at least a partial motive for the crime.
7) Many times killers with a clear motive for the intended death of another will either rob or sexually attack in the course of the crime. However, such adjunct acts are seen by the killer as nothing more than an added perk of the crime and not to be confused with being the actual primary motive for the crime. Thus, taking certain money from the register might have been nothing more than an afterthought by the killers.

Brown's Chicken Case: Final Analysis

It is reasonable and logical to take the position that the female owner of the store where Juan Luna had worked was the actual target of the crime. The circumstance in which the crime took lace may have been either intended or random, that is, the killers may have known in advance that multiple employees would be present or not. However, the fact that six other persons were present along with the intended victim certainly did act to obscure the actual motive for the mass murder. And until such time that criminal investigators correctly identify the primary motive for a killing, few if any such crimes are likely to be solved. As such, the presence of the additional six victims at the store clearly made case solution far more difficult than had the intended victim been alone at the time of her killing.

Case Note: Several months after the crime, this author was asked to offer his thoughts about the crime by a member of the homicide task force leading the police investigation. The author's response was brief: The female owner was killed in a personal manner while all the others were simply lined up and executed. Lynn Ehlenfeldt was the intended target. All the other victims were simply window-dressing.

Lane Bryant Case Overview

On February 2, 2008, five women were killed in a Lane Bryant store in Tinley Park, Illinois, a suburb south of Chicago. A sixth victim, a part-time employee of the store survived a graze wound to the neck and later supplied police investigators with her account of the crime.

The shorthand version of that account of events is that as the surviving victim and the store manager, Rhoda McFarland, were in the process of opening for the day, a lone black man walked into the store holding a piece of paper intimating that he was there to make a delivery. Moments later, he pulled a semi-automatic handgun and demanded funds from two cash registers. While this was going on, the first two customers of the day entered the store, following by two other customers immediately thereafter.

The lone gunman forced the six women into a back room and produced a role of duct tape and forced the victims to tape one another's hands after first having them remove valuables from each other's purses. The gunman left the women alone in the back room for a moment and Rhoda McFarland was able to use her cell phone and whispered for help from 911. The gunman returned and saw the call being made. He then shot McFarland once in the face and then shot the four customers one after the other in the back of their heads. He then shot the surviving victim, however, she would later state that she had been able to move her head as the shot rang out. The bullet allegedly intended for the back of her head simply grazed her neck.

---

### Investigating Survivors of Homicide Incidents

*There are those homicide investigations where one or more persons are murdered however other victims do survive the incident. Investigators immediately become reliant upon the survivors to provide a full account of events. Such witness accounts quickly become the basis for early violent crimes investigation. Such specifics as to the actions of the killer or killers typically provide much of the following information:*

*1) Accurate descriptions of the offenders;*
*2) Method of operation;*
*3) Possible or obvious motive for the crime;*
*4) Indications as to whether the crime was committed by strangers or by persons who knew the victims in life;*

5) *Descriptive identifiers gathered from offender statements; and*
6) *Specifics dealing with weapons, vehicles and possible items taken in the course of the crime.*

<u>*Analysis*</u>

*Such witness information often serves as the basis for effective and quick solutions to homicide investigations. To the extent that each above category contains accurate information, investigative leads abound. Though such specific information often allows violent crimes investigators with potential sources of places to carry out their inquiries, many such homicide investigations where victims survive with their lives become cold cases nonetheless.*

*Suppose that this discussion begins with an important reminder that individuals from all realms of life, including crime victims and witnesses, routinely lie to the police and other investigators. It is, therefore, a great investigative error for investigators to randomly accept an alleged witness account from the apparent survivor of violence that took the life of others. In the course of such investigative inquiries, one would do well to ask themselves certain or all of the following questions:*

1) *What was the apparent motive for the attack on the eventual murder victim?*

2)  *Under what circumstances was the surviving victim allowed to live?*

3)  *Was the survivor also attacked and either injured or left for dead?*

4)  *What possible motive might the survivor have to mislead the investigation, either by withholding certain information about the crime or by making actual untrue statements?*

5)  *After conducting a background information into the survivor's life, are there any apparent ways in which the survivor might stand to profit from the crime that resulted in the death of another?*

*The lone survivor described events and gave a description of a large black offender. Common sense criminal investigation calls for wondering certain things about the case.*

1)  *Why would the offender choose such an odd location and time to commit the crime?*

2)  *Why kill the victims ad allow a survivor to provide case information to the police?*

3)  *Does the manner in which the surviving victim describes the crime seem reasonable and logical?*

*This crime is notable for the senseless nature of the criminal behavior. The location of a department store with a parking lot 1,000 yards away is only a desirable location to commit a crime for one or two possible* reasons. *The first is that the bounty connected to the commission of the crime is potentially highly rewarding to the offenders, such as bags full of uncut jewels or kilos of uncut heroin. No such treasures were present in this crime. The second plausible reason for having chosen the victims inside the store is that one person among the victims was the actual target. Had only the intended target for death been gunned down, investigators would have likely correctly realized that fact. However, in this case where a half-dozen victims were executed side by side, the identity of the actual intended target becomes obscured.*

*The second question as to why the survivor lived now beckons. Was the killer's weapon empty of ammunition? Did the survivor take defensive measures to avoid having been gunned down alongside the non-survivors? Or did the killer have another reason not to kill the survivor?*

*As this case enters its second decade of going unsolved, one might consider that the crime is not what it appears to be. Written above was the fact that this crime seems highly notable for its apparent senseless aspects. Perhaps that statement needs to be modified to, "It is the description of events from the surviving victim that seems quite senseless."*

*One major task of accomplished violent crimes investigators is to assess known facts of a case, or supposed facts of a case, and subject that information to a theory or set of conditions by which many such events might occur.*

*The Misty Copsey Case affords an opportunity to create the framework of a theory that might explain what is thought or known to have happened. In this case, Misty's close friend and companion on the evening in question was Eve Knoll. A 14-year-old child at the time of Misty's disappearance, Eve was a homicide survivor if only in an indirect way, at least according to Eve's own accounts of events.*

*Eve Knoll stated the following to Misty Copsey's mother that same evening and repeated the same account to police investigators when they consented to investigate more than six months after the child-disappearance.*

1) *Eve said that Misty had missed the last bus of the evening toward her home in Spanaway.*
2) *Eve then called a 23-year-old friend named James Klimore to pick them up at the fair and drive both girls home.*
3) *Misty told Eve she would not get into Klimore's car.*
4) *Eve then called 18-year-old Pastor Schultz for a ride.*

*5)  Eve said at the time that she boarded her own bus heading in another direction toward her house, leaving Misty to be picked up by Schultz, or otherwise found her own way home.*

*Hours later Misty Copsey was gone.*

---

*As discussed above, bright police investigators weigh the account of case facts as given by surviving victims based on first having subjected what was said to investigative inquiry. In the Copsey Case, there is no indication that the police made any effort to verify anything Eve Knoll told them.*

*Some months later, a friend of both Misty and Eve contacted the police telling them that Eve had told her that she initially lied to the police and others when she said that she took the bus home from the fair when she left Misty behind. In actuality, Eve had gone ahead and taken a ride home from James Klimore after all.*

*The police did then interview Eve Knoll who admitted having lied to them during her first interview with them. The truth was that James Klimore had indeed picked her up at the fair and drove her home.*

*Of key importance is the fact that despite having learned that they had been successfully lied to by a mere child, the police apparently failed to follow up with* interrogating her to learn exactly what other lies she had previously told regarding the crime.

The reason for Eve Knoll having lied might have been simply because she did not want her guardian to know that she was seeing an adult with arrests for sexual assault and drug charges. Or the lies might have been of far greater consequence to the eventual solution to the case. What is certain from the viewpoint of an experienced investigator is that most 14-year-old children lack the nerve to lie to the police when the events turned deadly as in this case. Thus, there is every reason to assume that Eve Knoll lied about various other aspects of the Misty Copsey Case.

There is every reason to believe that Eve Knoll has made admissions to the actual facts of events on the evening in question to certain individuals. The location of such persons would lead to cold case investigators learning the truth. Lastly, it is important to keep in mind that Eve Knoll may have led a difficult life plagued by her conscience. She might put an end to such self-inflicted pain simply by telling the truth at this very late date.

---

Two men walked up to the customer service counter of a large supermarket and asked to fill out a discount card for future purchases. A young man waited on them and gave them the paper forms to be completed. Seconds later, the second employee finished working with another customer. The two men then calmly showed handguns in their waistbands and announced a robbery. The first employee handed over cash from the service drawer. The second female employee opened the safe and handed the gunmen several thousand dollars.

At that instant, the first employee made a furtive move reaching toward a pants pocket. One of the offenders shot that employee, killing him on the spot. They then ran from the store. The female victim survived the incident.

This case was a bit different than the others before it in the sense that a customer had witnessed much of what the surviving witness reported to the police. Both witness and victim saw the gunmen approach the customer service desk and the witness later saw the victims handing the proceeds over to the offenders.

Two issues were unclear from the point of the investigating police. Exactly why was the victim shot, as he had nothing in the pocket the offenders apparently thought he was reaching for, and why was the second victim able to survive the attack?

The surviving victim was questioned by the police. The investigative conclusion was that she seemed unduly nervous. She was *asked if she would be willing to submit to a polygraph test, however, she was not given the test as the particular investigators involved personally questioned the validity of the polygraph process.*

*The investigators then did a background check of the surviving victim. It was learned that she lived in the same residence as did a recently paroled ex-convict. A mugshot of the parolee was placed in a photo gallery and shown to the customer who had witnessed the incident. She identified that person as one of the offenders. The surviving victim was arrested, advised of her Miranda rights and interrogated. She admitted that she and her step-brother who had just been released from prison had planned the robbery. They also had enlisted the second gunman who was a friend of the family. The surviving victim and both gunmen were all charged with felony murder and armed robbery.*

*This case was solved within a matter of hours due to the investigative team having properly investigated the surviving victim of a homicide incident.*

---

Summary Comments on Surviving Victims

The Lane Bryant Case investigators have spent nine years investigating a mass murder based on what has been said to be the actual order of events of the crime, the killer's method of

300

operation and the physical description of the offender.

The alleged facts of the case have confused investigators, as many of the alleged actions of the killer seem not to make logical sense. It is for this reason that the actual crime motive remains obscure to many investigators and observers, and for as long as the motive remains in question, the case is unlikely to be solved.

Case analysis dictates that there are two possible reasons that the killer's actions seem odd – either the killer behaved illogically or the long pole information source provided authorities with inaccurate information.

<u>Surviving Victim Investigation Summary</u>

In at least one document written about the Lane Bryant Case, the surviving victim was referred to by the name "Martha." As a matter of convenience, that name will be used herein. It is to be noted that this analysis of two mass murder cases is based solely on the written word of others as this analyst has yet to conduct any allied investigations of either case. It is therefore important to understand that the author holds no opinions or theories that Martha was in any way complicit in this crime.

Rather, the piece written above regarding a potential involvement of certain surviving victims of murder events is presented as a general guideline for carrying out such case investigations. Consider the following:

1) The Lane Bryant investigators are likely to have spent literally thousands of hours investigating aspects of the case dealing with the sought-after suspect's physical description and method of operation.

2) Expert consultants rendered criminal profiles of the killer again, based on the accounts of the case supplied investigators by Martha.

3) Much of that information given the police by Martha makes little logical sense based on the manner in which she described the method of operation.

4) An investigative understanding of a killer's method of operation generally provides clarity in terms of understanding the actual motive for the crime.

5) Such analysis of method of operation in this case has served only to cause bright investigators ongoing confusion. The manner in which Martha says the offender acted makes no sense on countless fronts.

6) The above statements leads to one of two possible conclusions: (a) the killer has escaped detection despite his having not committed the crime in an intelligent manner; or (b) the crime did not actually occur as reported by the surviving victim.

---

For all these reasons, police investigators must conduct an in-depth investigation of Martha. It is important to consider that surviving victims may or may not have been acting with guilty knowledge in terms of the planning of the crime or it being carried out. General nice people, often without criminal histories, sometimes initiate future crimes simply by talking about their employment to friends or family who are themselves criminals. A simple comment about money or valuables being in a certain place at a certain time might provide a violent offender enough information to act on. In some such cases, the employee is told ahead of time that the offender plans a robbery or other such crime. Other times, the person known to the employee may simply show up at the place of employment and announce the crime. In either such situation, the surviving victim is unlikely to volunteer information to the police, either out of loyalty to the offender or out of fear of being charged themselves in the crime.

Means of Investigation

An experienced police interrogator might simply point out to the surviving victim the specific ways in which the witness's story is illogical and improbable. I homicide cases, the interrogator is wise to point out that the severity of the crime will result in long-term investigations likely to lead to case solution: "If you were in on this crime, we will find out," or "The sooner you cooperate and tell the truth, the better your chances are to control the damage." Similarly, interrogators often truthfully point out that authorities want to get the person who pulled the trigger more than they are concerned with accomplices to the crime.

Most bright investigators are not great advocates of polygraph testing simply because they are often inaccurate. However, when confronting a surviving victim, the mere threat of the lie detector may be sufficient to get then to tell the truth about the actual facts of the case.

Case Facts as per Surviving Victim

1) Police investigators are routinely taught early on to never accept an apparent coincidence as such until it is proven so. In this case, Martha claimed that she escaped execution by a .40 caliber pistol due to her good fortune of moving her head just as the trigger was being pulled. Only the police investigators actually know the crime scene setting in order to determine from physical evidence if the surviving victim's account of the shooting is plausible. The opposite way of attacking this issue is to determine if the killer might have been able to inflict a "graze wound" intentionally to alleviate police suspicion that Martha was complicit in the crime.

2) Police investigators surely have struggled from the beginning as to why Lane Bryant at opening time would have been a sensible target for robbery. The cash likely had no more than perhaps $200 each in order to make change for early customers.

3) The gunman is alleged to have waited for the four customers to enter the store in order to rob them. Suppose that any one of the shoppers left someone in their car directly in

front of the store. When they failed to return promptly they would have either gone inside the store to check on the customer or might have called them via cell phone. Either response might have caused a call to 911. Simply put, robberies occur quickly by design. Indications are that all six victims were detained by the gunman for perhaps as long as 20 minutes.

4) Lone robbers do not carry duct tape to their intended crime.

5) A gunman intent on carrying out a mass execution might well carry duct tape to their crime.

<u>Crime Investigative/Interrogation Intent</u>

The purpose of this analysis is not to suggest that the surviving victim actually knows more than she had said or that she is criminally involved in this case. Rather, the questioning of Martha and other investigative steps is to arrive at whatever the truth is. In the event that the police inquiry into the surviving witness clears her or any wrongdoing, they then know that as odd as the facts of the case might seem to be, that is actually what did take place. Investigators would no longer need to wonder if the actual killer is the same as what they were told. Similarly, if ballistics experts say that physical evidence supports that Martha had the good fortune to have moved her head as she was about the executed, then what she says took place becomes credible. Based on such investigative findings, investigators can move forward with the knowledge that they are indeed seeking a mass murderer as described by the surviving witness.

Moving Forward

Keep in mind that Martha might well have told the truth about every aspect of her report on the crime, yet the actual motive for the case may nonetheless have nothing to do with robbery. One of the usual primary tasks of investigators is to determine if the murder in question was the work of a stranger or of someone the victim knew in life. In a mass murder situation, the investigative task becomes multiplied by the number of victims. Any one of the five murder victims, as well as the surviving victim, may have been one of seven possible options. Any one of the separate women shot may have been the target while all of the others were killed for no other reason than to obscure the identity of the intended victim. Add to those six differing motives the unlikely possibility that the crime was actually an intended robbery and seven distinct avenues of investigations exist.

However, this larger number of possible intended victims becomes significantly reduced by the fact that the gunman was actually inside Lane Bryant with Rhoda McFarland and Martha before any of the customers arrived inside the store. In the event that one of the customers was the actual lone target, the gunman would have had to be armed with information that the intended victim was in fact going shopping at that store. However, from the offender's point of view, it would have been far smarter to wait outside until the arrival of the victim before allowing them to go inside the store.

It is once again important that analysts keep in mind that only by having all six victims present together inside the store that the identity of the actual intended victim becomes obscure.

A Motive Surfaces

Relationship murders are often solved by conducting an in-depth background investigation into the life of the victim. The result of conversations with persons who knew the victim well is that a motive for the crime surfaces. In the Lane Bryant Case, Rhoda McFarland, the store manager, had deep involvement in a religious order named Embassy Christian Center, which was led by a fellow named George Aja.

Rhoda McFarland herself was an ordained minister and had risen to the rank of associate pastor of the religious order some three years before the mass murder. Sometime in 2005, Aja took out a $900,000 mortgage on the church property that congregation members assumed was nearly paid off. Within only a matter of months of the disclosure of the mortgage loan, the congregation shrunk from 1,000 members to less than 100.

George Aja then moved his family to Austin, Texas, leaving the Illinois Embassy Christian Center in the hands of Rhoda McFarland. However, once Aja's financial activity came to her attention, she left the congregation.

Soon after the Lane Bryant mass murder, police investigators learned a former Embassy member made a 20-minute phone call one hour before the murders that was routed through the cell tower nearest the Lane Bryant store. It does not take investigative genius to theorize that the call was significant to the murders in one of two ways.

Theory I is that a friend of Rhoda McFarland called her with some important and likely alarming news connected to the congregation. It is quite possible that whatever the nature of the news, it in some way placed the victim in danger. Thus, a warning of danger to Rhoda McFarland would have been followed by her murder within an hour's time. Thus, the caller's information would have been capable of breaking the case.

Theory II is that the person connected to the congregation did not make the call to Rhoda McFarland but rather to an accomplice to discuss possible further action such as determining whether or not Rhoda would be showing up to Lane Bryant for work and how the party being called might respond in the event that the potential victim would soon arrive at Lane Bryant to work.

Whether theorists favor Theory I or II, the mere existence of a phone call from a former church member one hour before the crime is a prime example of an investigative lead capable of almost immediate case solution. In one case you have a witness who was friendly with Rhoda McFarland, who could tell police all about their fears and concerns in the hour before the crime. In the other case, the police have incriminating evidence that the phone conversation was for the purpose of planning the crime soon before its consummation. Armed with the identity of both the caller and the person called, the police have the investigative tools required to solve the crime.

If the cell phone call took place in any other way, it is a coincidence for the ages, and smart investigators do not believe in coincidences.

Investigative Note: This analysis is being written nine years after the Lane Bryant Case. The relevant information regarding the cell phone call clearly must have been obtained by the police long ago. Yet there has been no public declaration as to the findings of this investigative lead. Certainly, once the phone records were obtained, the resulting investigation should have been concluded in a relatively short period of time. One must wonder why the interested media would not have pushed for police disclosure into their findings regarding the cell phone call.

Similarly, dozens of police investigators traveled to Texas to investigate George Aja's Embassy Christian Center spin-off in that state. Clearly, the purpose of this investigation was to establish behaviors on Aja's part sufficient to act as a motive for murder. It is important to note that illegal behavior by George Aja does not suggest that the actual motive to have Rhoda McFarland killed would have been his alone. The mass murder could have actually been the work of any of scores of congregation "true believers" who might have wished to protect their cult-like secrets.

Final Lane Bryant Analysis

Accuracy in criminal investigative analysis should be based on objective reason and logic applied to known case facts. It is acknowledged here that without a viewing of the actual police files, this analysis is far more flimsy than one might wish it to be. However, relative probability shouts the following:

1) The killer carried duct tape to Lane Bryant not to rob but to kill Rhoda McFarland and anyone else who happened to be there.

2) The conspiracy to kill intended to obscure McFarland as the actual target for death by making her death one of many.

3) As in the Brown's Chicken Case, McFarland's would was different from the others – she was shot in the face so that the killer could actually witness her death. By contrast, the four customers were all executed by gunshot wounds to the back of their heads.

4) The cell phone call leading up to the mass murder was not coincidental. As stated above, it was either a warning to Rhoda McFarland or instruction to the killer.

5) The secrets to the actual motive for the crime rest with scores of past congregation members who know or suspect the truth.

6) The surviving victim, Martha, may have actually had a far closer relationship with Rhoda McFarland than suspected. Rhoda was

a nurse and Martha had recently started nursing school. Rhoda ministered to troubled young women and Martha had recently been devastated by an unexpected divorce. There may have been a relationship of trust there that may have led to other issues.

Comparative Case Analysis

Cases in which the motive is obscured by elements of the crime are difficult to solve. In both the Brown's Chicken Case and Lane Bryant Case, robbery likely did occur in the strictest sense in that a weapon was used to take month. However, the taking of funds was certainly not the primary motive for the resulting mass murders. To the respective gunmen, taking $100 or two simply supplied them with a bit of spending money while also causing the police to wrongly focus on robbery as a motive.

In the Brown's Chicken Case, Juan Luna and his accomplice entered the store waiving a handgun with the knowledge that the female owner would likely be there at closing time. Luna was a former employee who held a grudge against the owner, which served as a motive for his killing her. The fact that six other employees were also executed effectively acted to obscure his motive for having hilled her.

In the Lane Bryant Case, Rhoda McFarland knew damaging facts about past members of a religious organization where she had held the title of assistant pastor. The unknown specifics as to what was actually going on at the congregation might range from the actual commission of felony offenses to mere sexually compromising encounters capable of the destruction of marriages and religious reputations. Either such circumstance, or anything in between, might have served as a motive for murder.

Regardless of the specifics of the motive to kill Rhoda McFarland, the key factor is that the killers were convinced that Rhoda knew their dark secrets and they considered her as a looming threat to exposing them to what they considered to be potential ruin. So she had to go and therefore so did the others who unfortunately happened to be in the Lane Bryant store.